The Postage Stamps of Aden 1937 – 1968
2nd edition

Copyright 2022 Peter James Bond

PO Box 964
ROSNY PARK 7018
Tasmania
Australia

www.pjbond.com

ISBN 978-0-6487713-4-0

All rights reserved. No part of this publication may be reproduced, stored in
a retrieval system, or transmitted, in any form or by any means, electronic,
mechanical, photocopying, recording or otherwise (except under the statutory
exceptions provisions of the Australian *Copyright Act 1968*) without the prior
written permission of the publisher.

The Postage Stamps of Aden

1937 – 1968

2nd edition 2022

PETER JAMES BOND
PUBLISHER

Contents

Introduction 5

Collecting Aden 6

A Brief History of Aden 7

An Introduction to the Postal History of Aden 11

The Listings

    Colony of Aden / State of Aden 16

    Federation of South Arabia 30

    Kathiri State 34

    Mahra State 64

    Qu'aiti State 78

    State of Upper Yafa 105

Bibliography 115

1953 Aden 15c Coronation of Queen Elizabeth II, De La Rue imprint strip.

Introduction

2nd Edition

Publishing *The Postage Stamps of Aden 1937 – 1968* was an extension of my collecting interest. Over the years, several books have been dedicated to aspects of Aden philately. However, no recent titles provided an entire catalogue that included the later states' issues. The first edition of the book you now hold went into production in 2020. I was pleasantly surprised that it sold well. Clearly, many collectors find Aden a fascinating country.

No book is perfect, and one criticism of the first edition was that the illustrations weren't in colour. Printing in monochrome was intentional to keep the price down. However, colour printing is now more affordable, and this 2022 edition should please collectors who like their catalogue images at least approximating the actual stamps.

I entered the first edition in the 17th New Zealand National Philatelic Literature Exhibition, held in November 2021, at which it secured a Silver Award. The judges' critique was encouraging, and their suggestions have been incorporated into this new edition.

◆

Scope

This handbook is primarily concerned with the stamps of Aden, but its postal history can not be ignored. Much has been published about this fascinating subject. Collectors may be aware of India-used-in-Aden stamps and perhaps have an example in their album, but the topic is broad and complex. Before the stamp listings, an introduction is included to familiarise collectors with Aden's postal history.

As well as Aden, the protectorate states' stamps are listed in full, despite the postal validity of later issues being in question. Collectors can decide their own chronological endpoint. The various Yemen issues are outside the scope of this book.

◆

Values

This publication is a guide rather than a catalogue, and the editor/publisher is not a stamp dealer. So it is definitely not a price list.

The concept of 'catalogue value' today is well understood by stamp collectors. In years gone by, a catalogue was actually a list of selling prices of the publisher, who was also a stamp dealer. Modern business models provide that the publisher and the dealer are often separate entities. Most dealers now see catalogue values as a place to start discounting their stock, though sometimes the market outpaces publications, and 'real' prices are higher.

The values quoted here are mostly typical selling prices, which you could expect to pay a seller, usually online. Some scarcer items are either not afforded a value or one that has been inferred by similar material. As always, condition is a great leveller and, particularly with the 1937 Dhow issue, the value of used higher denominations will vary. No value has been apportioned where it has proven impossible to determine a typical selling price.

It is worth noting that the later states' issues of imperforate miniature sheets are often encountered online with selling prices over $100. These are often sold for lower prices, which is reflected in this publication. As with all stamps listed here, there is a bias towards valuations at the lower end of the market.

This book is published in Australia, though marketed worldwide. Values are quoted in pounds sterling and US dollars as this convention broadly appeals to international collectors. American readers are asked to excuse the otherwise British nature of the presentation. You will see unfamiliar spelling such as colour, catalogue, grey etc., and dates expressed in day-month-year format.

◆

Collecting Aden

Why collect Aden? Why a stamp collector concentrates on one country or another is often a matter of circumstance rather than a planned strategy. My case is probably typical of many collectors. Perhaps it strikes a familiar chord with you. As a six-year-old, I collected stamps for no better reason than because my older brother did. With no money to buy specimens for my album – a welcome Christmas present – I collected anything that came my way, although accumulated would undoubtedly be a more accurate word.

As time passed, my collecting became more structured. Thus, my whole world approach was narrowed down to a British Commonwealth collection. Later, that too was restricted to Australia and Australian dependencies. The boyhood 'foreign' collection had long gone, swapped for more exciting treasures, but the Commonwealth album still lurked in a drawer, waiting to be rediscovered.

As I tired of Australia, thanks to having reached completion so far as my budget would allow, I looked elsewhere. My old Commonwealth album resurfaced, and I noticed a few countries were better represented than others. The first one was Aden. Here lies one of that colony's advantages. Until 1964, it was the first country, alphabetically, in the Stanley Gibbons catalogue. Abu Dhabi has since relegated Aden to second place.

I soon discovered why Aden was to the west of Australia, despite being in the middle east and why the far east was to our north. The educational benefit of stamp collecting was apparent even then. As you would appreciate, part-sets in an album are anathema to a collector, and those spaces had to be filled. Once the sets were complete, those totally absent had to be found, so it continued. By degrees, I collected Aden, if not exclusively, certainly more passionately than other countries, quite by chance.

Of course, the stamps of Aden hold much appeal. Simultaneously they can be terribly British and exotically foreign. They are familiar and unusual, offer definitive and commemorative, historical and pictorial, common and rare. You can settle for cheap and cheerful or track down the more exclusive (read expensive) rarities. Traditional collectors hold Aden dear, while thematic collectors find a wide range of subjects in Aden's arsenal.

The Aden catalogue contains several scarce and, therefore, valuable stamps. However, collectors on a limited budget can readily put together a comprehensive and solidly representative collection without the annoyance of too many gaps. Furthermore, Aden may readily be divided into historical and geographical entities, which is convenient to the collector who wishes to concentrate on one sector without the unwanted arbitrary 'ruling off' of the catalogue.

In my case, the want of an example or two of Indian stamps used in Aden ended up a modest collection in its own right and is still growing. However, I must add that the scarcer, more expensive items still elude me. Luxuries like food and household bills seem to want to come first.

One benefit not lost on the Aden collector of today is that there are no new issues, though I dare say you could attempt to continue the theme with Yemen if you wished. While a steady trickle of new stamps through the year can be a pleasant enough experience, many countries' annual issues prove to be a costly exercise. 'Dead' countries have an appeal all their own, not only for that reason.

So, from India used in Aden and all its fascinating permutations, we can progress to the mid-sixties with the states' varied and colourful issues. While many of the latter are not afforded entries in mainstream catalogues, some specialist publications offer the collector a guide. The keyword there is 'guide'. Without an authoritative record, one can merely speculate whether an overprint in red ink rather than blue is worth $1500, or perhaps only $15. The philatelic market has to use the tried and trusted supply/demand formula to establish an item's actual value, rather than a published price, which can be two entirely different things.

Catalogue status means different things to different people. Some collect only according to Gibbons or Scott, while others will buy whatever was issued, notwithstanding postal validity, contemporary availability or usage. The plethora of issues depicting paintings, Olympic and space motifs from the Aden states between 1966 and 1968 were unnecessary and aimed solely at collectors' wallets. However, compared to many countries' current philatelic outputs, the later Kathiri, Qu'aiti, Mahra, and Upper Yafa efforts might be considered modest.

It boils down to deciding what your focus is. Whether it be bona fide stamp issues or the broader philatelic story, above all, enjoy your Aden collection.

◆

A Brief History of Aden

The history of Aden is a long story. Most stamp collectors concern themselves only with the years from 1937 when the first Aden postage stamps were issued. However, intrepid postal history enthusiasts will start in the middle of the 19th century, when Indian stamps franked mail from this outpost of the British empire on the southern tip of Arabia.

While the Aden story goes back centuries, much of it comprises myths and legends, which intriguingly may have some element of fact. The port's location made it useful as a shipping stop-off point, and it is recorded that it saw trading activity between India and Red Sea destinations. The 1st century AD *Periplus of the Erythraean Sea*[1] mentioned Aden as 'a village by the sea,' possibly describing what is now called Crater.

---

1 *Periplus of the Erythraean Sea* is a Greco-Roman document describing navigation and trading locations along the Red Sea coast, the Horn of Africa and the Arabian Sea.

The Himyarite (or Homerite) Kingdom was a nation in ancient Yemen. Dating from 110BC, its capital was the city of Zafar until the 4th century. It was then replaced by what is now Sana'a. Various conflicts resulted in the Himyars annexing, among others, the Hadhramaut region around 300AD. The first recorded fortifications of Aden were built in this period.

In the 10th century, most of Aden's population were Persians. However, from the 12th century, when robust building commenced, Aden was regularly visited by merchants from Egypt, the east coast of Africa and as far afield as China.

In 1421, China's Ming dynasty Emperor Yongle despatched a fleet of three ships to Aden, perhaps the first such official state visit to the area. Almost a century later, in 1513, Portugal laid siege to Aden. The assault lasted only four days, but Portugal persisted and ruled Aden for many years in the 16th century. The strategic significance of the port's position was being recognised. In 1538, the Ottomans occupied it though their interest was more to prevent European incursion than a point of control for trade. The Ottoman Empire governed Aden until 1645.

The first British appearance in Aden, in 1609, was a visit by the ship *Ascension* en route to Mocha on the Red Sea coast of Yemen. Following the departure of the Ottomans, Aden was ruled by the Sultanate of Lahej. For several months in 1796, a British fleet docked at Aden as a convenient base during Britain's war with France. When the French were defeated in Egypt in 1801, the Royal Navy spent many subsequent years hunting down French privateers.

The permanent population of Aden in 1800 was about 600. At this time, little British trade was undertaken, and the government, for the most part, took almost no interest in the region. However, some politicians, as well as East India Company management, feared further French incursions. The Governor of Bombay argued that India should be protected from foreign interests, including Russia, by capturing 'places of strength' to defend the Indian Ocean. In 1838, the Sultan of Lahej ceded 194 km2, including the port of Aden, to Great Britain. On 19 January 1839, Royal Marines were landed at Aden by the British East India Company to occupy the territory.

In 1937, Aden was detached from India and became the British Crown **Colony of Aden**. The region surrounding the colony, and Hadhramaut, were declared the Aden Protectorate and governed from Aden proper.

A typically British perspective of Aden is reflected in this extract of an article published in 1949[2] when the population exceeded 80,000:

> Travellers to India whose ship puts in at the Port of Aden for refuelling might well be excused if they take but one glance at that bare and rocky peninsula sweltering in the noon-day heat and turn hastily away to seek iced drinks in the bar. If they should prove more intrepid and venture ashore, it is fairly certain that on their return, the phrase 'God-forsaken hole' will figure at least once in their conversation.
>
> Aden has been a colony only since 1937, when the territory was taken from the control of the Government of India and its entry into the stamp issuing countries of the empire was marked by the famous Dhow set, one of the scarcest of the moderns. Not until 1942, however, were stamps issued for two of the native sultanates, both in the eastern Aden protectorate – the Qu'aiti State of Shihr and Mukalla, and the Kathiri State of Seiyun.

---

2   *The Philatelic Magazine*, 22 July 1949.

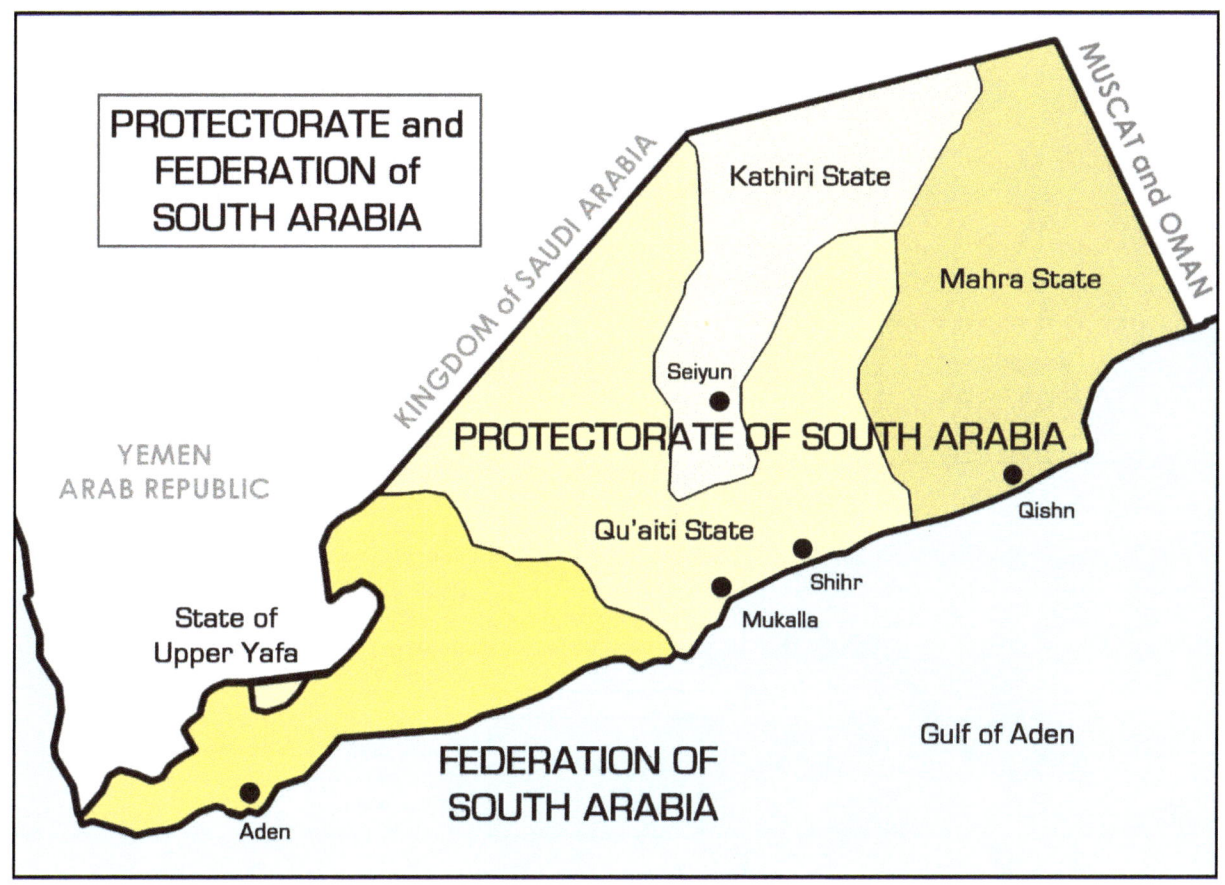

This Eastern Protectorate extends right to the western boundary of the Sultanate of Muscat and Oman. It includes the wild region of the Hadhramaut, which has been so graphically described and illustrated in the books of Miss Freya Stark. Incidentally, it may interest readers to know that the beautifully engraved issues of 1942 were based on Miss Stark's photographs.

The Federation of South Arabia was created on 4 April 1962. It was an association of states under British protection. In 1963, it was merged with the Colony of Aden, which was renamed the State of Aden. Another state was included in 1964 to take the Federation to 17 states. The Protectorate of South Arabia was formally established in 1963 and comprised the states that chose not to join the Federation. The four stamp-issuing states were Kathiri, Mahra, Qu'aiti and Upper Yafa. The first three constituted the Eastern Protectorate, and Upper Yafa was located in the Western Protectorate.

The Federation and Protectorate ceased to exist on 30 November 1967. The entire region was reconstituted as the People's Republic of Southern Yemen, which was renamed the People's Democratic Republic of Yemen in 1970. This entity was a Marxist socialist republic under the aegis of the USSR. Following the collapse of communism in Europe in 1990, it merged with the Yemen Arab Republic to form the Republic of Yemen. The political and stamp issuing complexity of Aden is more easily

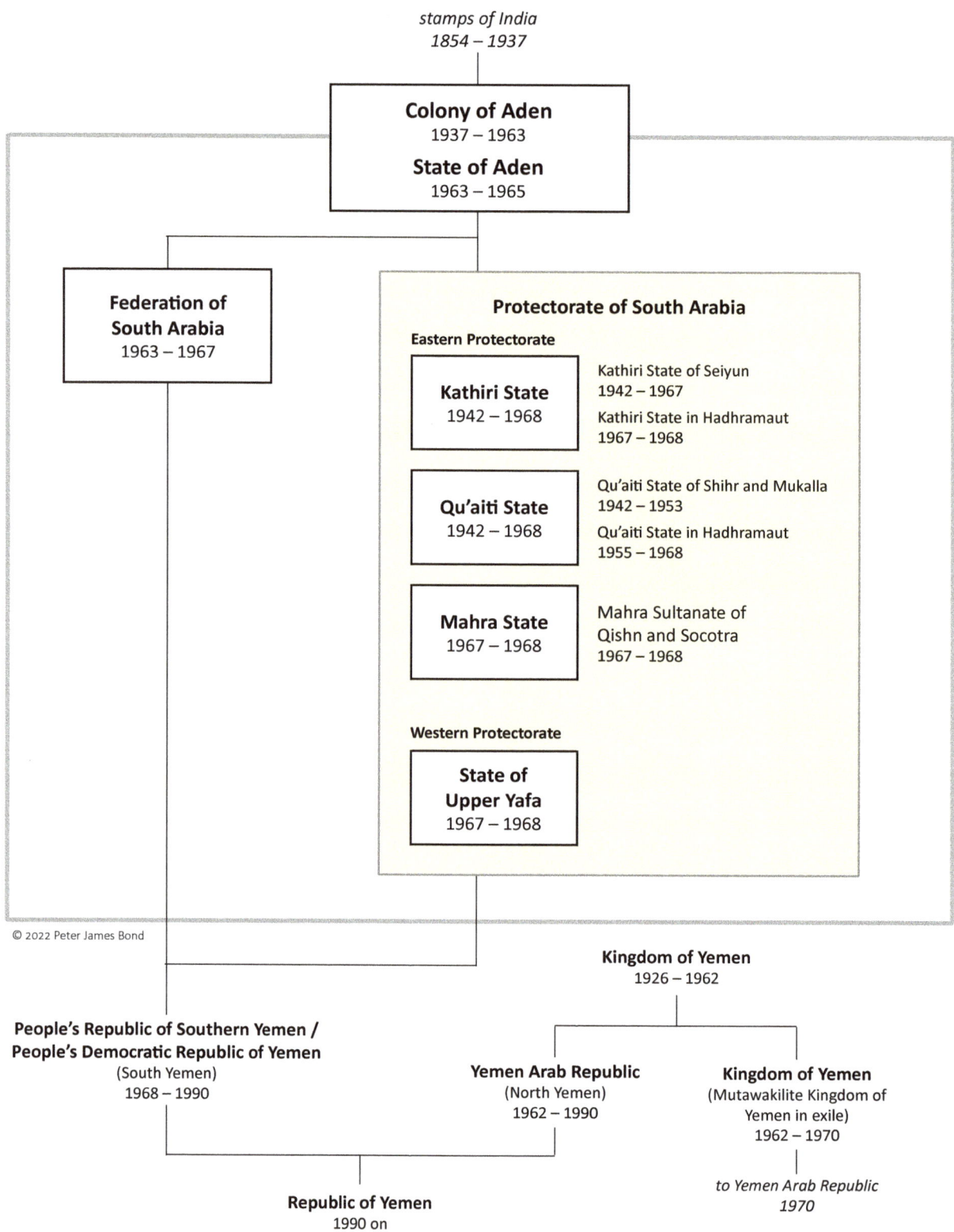

understood if viewed graphically. The accompanying chart should assist collectors in grasping the situation. Protectorate stamp issues continued after 1967, and Stanley Gibbons notes that:

> The government of the Southern Yemen Republic repudiated a contract under which the former rulers authorised some further new issues which were placed on the market. However ... there is some uncertainty as to whether any of these later issues were delivered and actually used for postal purposes.

◆

An Introduction to the Postal History of Aden

As with many countries, the postal history of Aden partly reflects its growth and changes in governance. Before the 1830s, that development was slow, and the gradual interest shown by European powers barely impacted the region. However, the British naval and military occupation on 19 January 1839 was a pivotal moment in Aden's story. The harbour was an ideal stop-off for shipping, and a mail service was quickly implemented.

The earliest surviving mail item is dated 15 June 1839, sent by one James Burns, a private in the Bombay European Regiment. His letter, which described the attack and capture of Aden, would most likely have been posted at Crater, where an office was maintained by the Assistant Political Resident. Mail from here was taken to Steamer Point by camel for onforwarding.

The earliest mail out of Aden was hand stamped with an India Oval Soldier 3 marking, and on arrival, with a small India F circular postmark. The oldest surviving 'Aden' postmarked mail dates from 1841, and by 1855 six different designs were in use. These were:

Rectangular
1. Aden Bearing – used by contract ships other than P&O.
2. Aden Paid – used by contract ships other than P&O.
3. Aden Shipletter Bearing – used by non-contract ships.
4. Aden Shipletter Paid – used by non-contract ships.

Circular
5. Aden BPP Bearing – used by P&O contract ships.
6. Aden BPP Paid – used by P&O contract ships.

Fig. 1   Fig. 2   Fig. 3   Fig. 4

Fig.5 Fig. 6 Fig. 7 Fig. 8

Note: BPP = British Packet Postage

Thought to have been introduced after the issue of Indian postage stamps in 1854 is the boxed INDIA PAID marking (Fig. 7). However, only a handful of examples are known, on mail passing through Aden from Mauritius or Reunion. Prepayment of postage on correspondence to the United Kingdom became compulsory in 1858. This requirement applied to other countries four years later. From 1859 till 1862, mail for which postage was to be paid on arrival was identified with a boxed INDIA UNPAID marking (Fig. 8).

India's first postage stamps were issued in 1854, and their use on Aden postal items is recorded from 1855. The earliest surviving cover is from March of that year, with the stamp cancelled by a diamond of dots (Fig. 9). This canceller was in general use in India, so items emanating from Aden require other postal markings to correctly identify them. The diamond of dots cancel was replaced in 1855 with the barred 124 postmark (Fig. 10). This canceller identifies Aden as post office number 124 of India's Bombay presidency. Covers are known backstamped with a double-circle postmark (Fig. 11).

By 1857 the administration of postal services was taken over by a postmaster, relieving the Assistant Political Resident of the task. Increased mail volumes led to the establishment of a post office at Steamer Point. Dedicated circular date stamps (Fig. 12) were used in conjunction with the barred 124 canceller. Later, the head post office was transferred from Crater to Steamer Point. The latter's accommodation was a mud and plaster building. This soon proved inadequate, and a larger building was completed in 1868. Finally, Crater was demoted to a branch office.

Collectors will find stamps other than Indian with the 124 or other Aden postmarks. Ceylon and Mauritius are reasonably common, but the cancels are also known on stamps of Great Britain, New South Wales, Canada, Switzerland, and French colonial issues. This situation could have occurred for various reasons. Typically, letters may have been prepared by a ship's passenger at a port of

Fig. 9 Fig. 10a Fig. 10b Fig. 11 Fig. 12

embarkation or stop-off point, then posted in Aden. A convoluted process of sending telegrams also saw British stamps postmarked with the 124 canceller.

From 1868 two types of duplex postmark (Fig's. 13 – 15) were introduced, apparently on an experimental basis. They are considered very rare. This period presents a complex series of postmarks, not all of which are illustrated here. That is a subject for a more detailed presentation. However, one aspect should be pointed out: postmarks of the period were produced with serifed and non-serifed lettering. Cantonment refers to either a temporary or permanent military camp.

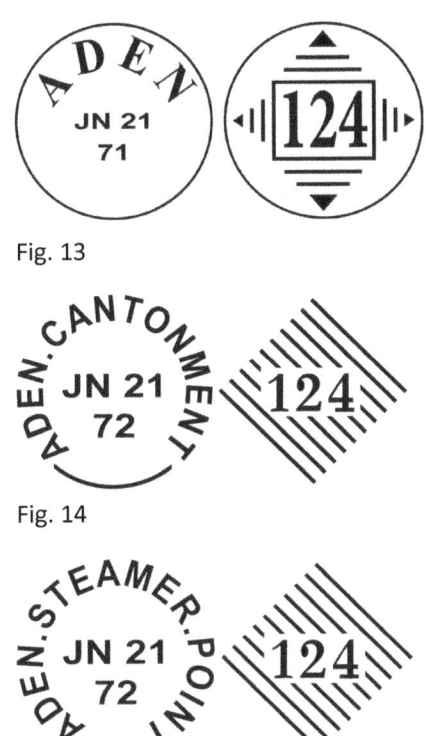

Fig. 13

Fig. 14

Fig 15

In 1872 India implemented a new post office identification system. Previously, post offices within each administration (presidency) were allocated a three-digit number, such as 124 used in Aden. While this method worked satisfactorily for a time, the proliferation of offices and sub-offices throughout India demanded an improved, uniform arrangement. Major Richard Pratt states, 'by 1868, there were four or five offices spread across India using the same obliteration number.'

The new 'All India Series' resulted in Aden being allocated number B-22 (Fig. 17), the letter indicating the Bombay Presidency. Aden Cantonment at Crater was assigned B-22 1 (Fig. 19). However, with about 100,000 post offices in India, this system became unworkable. Therefore, the numeric B cancellers were withdrawn and replaced with a similar obliterator which included only the initial of the presidency. Consequently, Aden and Aden Cantonment were provided with a canceller displaying only the letter B (Fig. 20). Each postmark was usually applied in conjunction with a simple circular date stamp (Fig. 16 and 18). These types were used separately and in duplex format, the former being rare.

The *Indian Postal Manual* of 1873 stipulated that it was unnecessary to include the year in the dateline of postmarks. This policy lasted until 1884, and collectors find it difficult to date covers of the period unless identified with other postal markings. Also, at this time, Aden Cantonment became known as

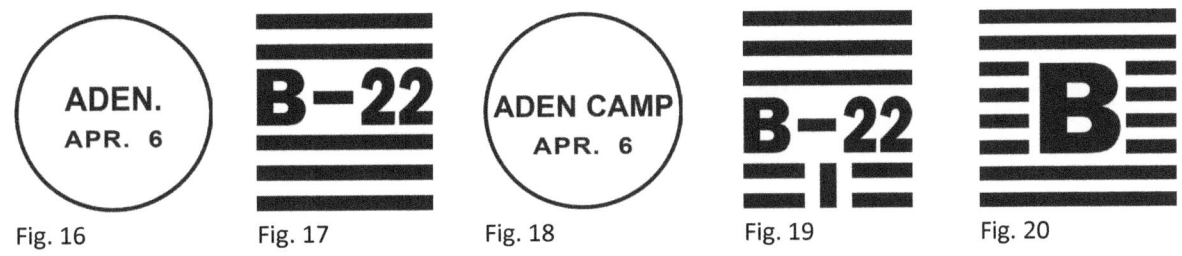

Fig. 16　　Fig. 17　　Fig. 18　　Fig. 19　　Fig. 20

Aden Camp. Usage of both names and the abbreviated Aden Cant persisted until 1894, when Aden Camp was decisively adopted. A fourth barred B canceller was used at two British Somaliland post offices, then administered by the Aden Postmaster. This circular design was later used at the Sheikh Othman and Khormaksar sub-post offices.

About 1884, the B obliterators were replaced by a new design. The squared circle postmark (Fig. 21) appeared in five types:

1. Aden with four-bar corners
2. Aden with three-bar corners (small lettering)
3. Aden with three-bar corners (large lettering)
4. Aden Cantonment
5. Aden Camp.

The Aden Camp cancel is notably larger than the others. The squared circle postmarks were replaced in the 1890s by a series of single or double circles.

Other post offices were opened in Aden from 1887 to 1937, some of which were closed after a short time:

1887-1903	Berbera (located in British Somaliland)
1887-1903	Zaila (located in British Somaliland)
1891-1915; 1922-1937	Sheikh Othman
1892-1915; reopened 1925	Khormaksar
1903-1904	Experimental Post Office B-84 (renamed Dthali) (Fig. 22)
1904-1907	Dthali (Fig. 23)
1904-1905	Nobat-Dakim (used the B-84 postmark)
1915	Kamaran
1915-1936	Perim (Fig. 24)
1924	Maalla.

Fig. 21

Fig. 22

Fig. 23

Fig. 24

Some of these offices used postmarks that followed the design of the Khormaksar example above. However, other formats were also issued. The Perim postmark is unique in that the town name was not incorporated into the double circle. It also has two date settings, one narrow (pictured) and the other a wider setting. The pre-stamp period includes one notable slogan cancellation, advocating support for the King George V Jubilee Fund (Fig. 25).

Aden's postal history is ongoing. It didn't end with the issue of its first stamps, on 1 April 1937. Many collectors concentrate on the nineteenth century, though for many more, covers from this period are too expensive to procure. The later India-used-in-Aden material is more accessible, and a representative collection can be assembled for a modest outlay. Changes in postmark design (Fig. 26-28) can add a fascinating insight. The benefit of collecting postal history is that there is no standard catalogue to tell you that your collection is incomplete.

This brief introduction to Aden's fascinating postal history is intended to whet the appetites of those who may have previously been interested only in the country's postage stamps. Other published works provide far more information than is provided here. Specialists can select from several areas to explore: concession mail, transit mail, airmail, maritime mail (including paquebot), registered mail, field post offices, and base offices.

Fig. 25

Fig. 26

Fig. 27

Fig. 28

Notes:

1. Most of the postmark illustrations presented here have been digitally enhanced or are digital reconstructions created in the interests of clarity. The typefaces depicted are close approximations to those used on the original cancellations and should not be regarded as historically accurate.

2. References:
   The Postal History of British Aden (1839-1967)
       - Major R.W. Pratt (editor Edward B. Proud), 1985
   The Postal History of Aden and Somaliland Protectorate
       - Edward B. Proud, 2005
   The Postal History of Aden 1839-1937
       - J.L.R. Croft, London Philatelist, Volume 76, July to October 1967.
   Aden 1839-1954
       - Major Richard Pratt, Gibbons Stamp Monthly, Volume 4 Number 11, April 1974
   Aden and its States 1840-1954
       - Major R.W. Pratt, London Philatelist Volume 83, July to October 1974.
   The Dhow (journal)
       - Aden and Somaliland Study Group, issues from February 2000.
   Checklist of Postmarks and Postage Stamps used at Aden during the 19th Century
       - Liane and Sergio Sismondo, www.sismondostamps.com/infobyte/Aden1.htm

◆

Colony of Aden

1937 – 1963

State of Aden

1963 – 1965

The stamps of Aden can be neatly divided into King George VI and Queen Elizabeth II issues. Many of the commemoratives are part of British Commonwealth omnibus series and, while not being reflective of the history or culture of Aden, provide a colourful and interesting aspect for the collector.

The 1937 Dhow definitive set is notable as a very early issue of the reign of George VI, predating the king's first British definitives by six weeks.

In the listings that follow, the 1939 series identifies many colour shades. These create a dilemma for the collector, as distinguishing one from another is a subjective, comparative process. Dated postmarks may help for used examples, but shades on mint stamps are more accurately identified with a side-by-side analysis.

King George VI

1 – 12	1937	Definitives – Dhow
13 – 15	1937	Coronation of King George VI
16 – 28	1939	Definitives – King George VI
29 – 30	1945	Victory
31 – 32	1948	Silver Wedding
33 – 36	1948	75th Anniversary of UPU
37 – 47	1951	Definitives – New Currency

Queen Elizabeth II

48	1953	Coronation of Queen Elizabeth II
49 – 60	1953	Definitives – Queen Elizabeth II
61	1954	Royal Visit
62 – 74	1954-62	Definitives – Queen Elizabeth II
75 – 76	1959	Revised Constitution
77	1963	Freedom from Hunger
78 – 87	1964	Definitives – Queen Elizabeth II

1937   Definitives – Dhow

1 April 1937

Printer: De La Rue
Watermark: Multiple script CA (sideways)
Perforation: 13 x 11.75

			£ MNH	£ FU/CTO	$US MNH	$US FU/CTO
1	½A	yellow-green	3.00	1.75	3.75	2.25
2	9p	deep green	3.00	2.00	3.75	2.50
3	1A	sepia	2.50	1.25	3.25	1.60
4	2A	scarlet	3.75	3.00	4.75	3.75
5	2½A	bright blue	5.00	1.50	6.25	2.00
6	3A	carmine	6.75	4.75	8.50	6.00
7	3½A	grey-blue	5.50	3.25	7.00	4.00
8	8A	pale purple	17.00	7.50	20.00	9.50
9	1R	brown	37.50	7.50	50.00	9.50
10	2R	yellow	75.00	22.50	95.00	28.00
11	5R	deep purple	£190	75.00	$240	95.00
a		... bright aniline purple	£275	£100	$340	$125
12	10R	olive-green	£475	£375	$600	$475
1/12		set of 12	£750	£450	$950	$550
S		... perforated SPECIMEN	£500	–	$625	–

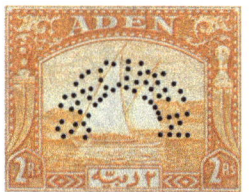

12   10S – SPECIMEN

1937   Coronation of King George VI

12 May 1937

Printer: De La Rue
Watermark: Multiple Script CA
Perforation: 13.75 x 14

13	1A	sepia	1.00	.75	1.25	1.00
a		… broken bar in A of left value tablet (R15/4)				
b		… damaged E of ADEN (R14/3)				
14	2½A	light blue	1.25	1.00	1.50	1.25
a		… watermark inverted	£2000	£2000	$2,500	$2,500
15	3½A	grey-blue	1.50	1.25	2.00	1.50
13/15		set of 3	3.00	2.25	3.75	2.75
S		… perforated SPECIMEN	80.00	–	$100	–

13   14   15

13a – broken bar in A   13b – damaged E   14S – SPECIMEN

1939   Definitives – King George VI

19 January 1939

Printer: Waterlow & Sons
Watermark: Multiple Script CA
Perforation: 12.5

The shades listed are as identified in *The Potter-Shelton Tables of K.G. VI Printings* and other sources. Additional printings of identical shades are not listed here. No attempt has been made to value the various shades printed for this issue.

					£ MNH	£ FU/CTO	$US MNH	$US FU/CTO
16	½A	yellowish green			1.50	.25	2.00	.30
	a	... paler yellow-green	Jul 42					
	b	... lighter green	Jan 44					
	c	... deeper green	Jun 45					
	d	... bluer green	Sep 48					
	e	... slightly deeper blue-green	Jan 50					
	f	... blue-green	May 50					
	g	... deep blue-green	May 51					
17	¾A	red-brown			2.00	.50	2.50	.70
	a	... deep red-brown	Jan 44					
	b	... colder red-brown	May 50					
18	1A	pale blue			1.25	.20	1.50	.25
	a	... pale ultramarine	Jul 42					
	b	... deeper ultramarine	Jan 44					
	c	... brighter ultramarine	48					
	d	... brighter blue	Nov 50					
	e	... bright blue	Mar 52					
19	1½A	scarlet			2.00	.25	2.50	.30
	a	... deeper scarlet	Jan 44					
	b	... brighter scarlet	Apr 47					
	c	... paler scarlet	48					
	d	... rose-scarlet	Jan 50					
20	2A	sepia			1.30	.10	1.60	.15
	a	... paler sepia	Jul 42					
	b	... grey-brown	Jan 44					
	c	... greyer brown	Apr 46					
	d	... cold grey-brown	Apr 47					
	e	... cold sepia	Jan 50					
	f	... greyish sepia	May 50					
	g	... grey sepia	Mar 52					
21	2½A	deep ultramarine			1.30	.15	1.60	.20
	a	... brighter deep ultramarine	May 50					
22	3A	sepia & carmine			1.30	.10	1.60	.15
	a	... sepia & bright carmine	Jul 42					
	b	... sepia & deep carmine	Jan 44					
	c	... sepia & deeper carmine	Jan 45					
	d	... deep sepia & deep carmine	Jun 45					
	e	... sepia & paler carmine	Nov 50					
	f	... sepia & rose	Mar 52					
23	8A	red-orange			1.75	.20	2.00	.25
	a	... deeper red-orange	Jan 44					
	b	... paler red-orange	Feb 48					
	c	... redder orange	Nov 50					
24	14A	sepia & light blue	15 Jan 45		3.25	.40	4.00	0.50
	a	... deeper sepia & light blue	Jun 45					
	b	... sepia & dull blue	Jul 47					
	c	... deeper sepia & bright blue	48					
25	1R	emerald-green			3.50	1.25	4.50	1.50
	a	... paler emerald	Jan 44					
	b	... deeper emerald	Jul 44					

23S – SPECIMEN

	c		... emerald	Jun 45			
	d		... brighter emerald	Apr 46			
	e		... pale emerald	Mar 52			
26		2R	deep indigo & magenta		9.00	1.50	11.00	1.75
	a		... indigo & bright magenta	Jan 44			
	b		... paler indigo & magenta	Apr 46			
	c		... blue-black & magenta	Mar 52			
27		5R	red-brown & olive green		26.00	7.25	33.00	9.00
	a		... red-brown & deeper olive	Jan 44			
	b		... paler colours	Oct 49			
28		10R	sepia & violet		33.00	7.50	40.00	9.50
	a		... darker sepia & brighter violet	Jan 44			
	b		... deep sepia & bright violet	Jan 50			
16/28			set of 13		80.00	17.00	$100	21.00
	S		... perforated SPECIMEN		£125	–	$150	–

			£ MNH	£ FU/CTO	$US MNH	$US FU/CTO
1946	**Victory**					
	15 October 1946					
Printer:	De La Rue					
Watermark:	Multiple Script CA					
Perforation:	13.75 x 14					
29	1½A	carmine	.65	.75	.75	1.00
a		… accent over D of ADEN				
30	2½A	blue	.65	.75	.75	1.00
a		… watermark inverted	£1500		$1800	
29/30		set of 2	1.20	1.40	1.40	1.75
S		… perforated SPECIMEN	£110	–	$140	–

29

29a – accent over D of ADEN

30

			£ MNH	£ FU/CTO	$US MNH	$US FU/CTO
1949	**Silver Wedding**					
	17 January 1949					
Printer:	1½A – Waterlow & Sons					
	10R – Bradbury, Wilkinson					
Watermark:	Multiple Script CA					
Perforation:	1½A – 14 x 14.75					
	10R – 11.5 x 10.75					
31	1½A	scarlet	.80	1.10	1.00	1.40
a		… flaw on 4 and 8 of 1948 (R2/6)	40.00	40.00	50.00	50.00
32	10R	mauve	30.00	32.00	35.00	38.00
31/32		set of 2	30.00	32.00	35.00	38.00

31

31a – flaw on 4 and 8

32

			£ MNH	£ FU/CTO	$US MNH	$US FU/CTO

1949   75th Anniversary of UPU

10 October 1949

Printer: 2½A and 1R – Waterlow & Sons
3A and 8A – Bradbury, Wilkinson
Surcharges – Waterlow & Sons
Watermark: Multiple Script CA
Perforation: 2½A and 1R – 13.7 to 13.9
3A and 8A – 10.75 x 11.5

			£ MNH	£ FU/CTO	$US MNH	$US FU/CTO
33	2½A on 20c	ultramarine	.40	.90	.50	1.10
34	3A on 30c	carmine-red	1.25	.90	1.60	1.10
35	8A on 50c	orange	1.25	1.20	1.60	1.50
a		... C of CA omitted from watermark	£1000		$1250	
36	1R on 1/-	blue	1.00	3.25	1.25	4.00
33/36		set of 4	3.50	5.50	4.50	6.75

33   34

35   36

1951   Definitives – New Currency

1 October 1951

Printer: Waterlow & Sons
Watermark: Multiple Script CA
Perforation: 12.5

			£ MNH	£ FU/CTO	$US MNH	$US FU/CTO
37	5c on 1A	light blue	.20	.25	.25	.30
a		... bright light blue				
38	10c on 2A	sepia	.15	.25	.20	.30
a		... brown sepia				
b		... deep sepia				
39	15c on 2½A	deep ultramarine	.30	.75	.40	1.00
a		... surcharge double	£1000		$1250	
40	20c on 3A	sepia & carmine	.25	.25	.30	.30
a		... dark sepia & carmine rose				

				£ MNH	£ FU/CTO	$US MNH	$US FU/CTO
41	30c on 8A		red-orange	.50	.40	.65	.50
42	50c on 8A		red-orange	1.00	.20	1.25	.25
	a		... surcharge double, one albino	£2250		$2800	
43	70c on 14A		sepia & pale blue	1.25	.90	1.50	1.10
	a		... dark sepia & bright pale blue				
44	1/- on 1R		emerald-green	1.75	.20	2.00	.25
45	2/- on 2R		indigo & magenta	8.50	2.25	10.00	2.75
	a		... surcharge omitted (albino)	£950		$1200	
	b		... blue-black & magenta				
46	5/- on 5R		red-brown & olive-green	16.00	10.00	20.00	12.50
	a		... red-brown & sage green				
47	10/- on 10R		sepia & violet	22.00	10.00	27.00	12.50
37/47			set of 11	45.00	22.50	55.00	28.00

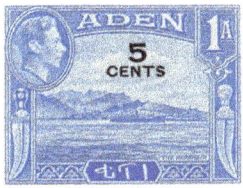   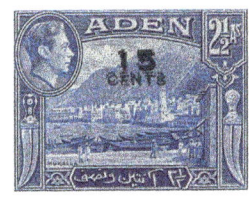

37   38   39   39a

   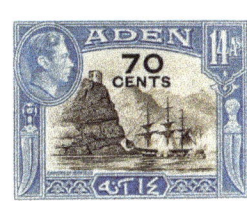

40   41   42   43

  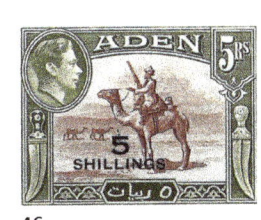 

44   45   46   47

1953   Coronation of Queen Elizabeth II

2 June 1953

Printer: De La Rue
Watermark: Multiple Script CA
Perforation: 13.5 x 13

48	15c	black & green	1.10	1.10	1.40	1.40

48

61

1953   Definitives – Queen Elizabeth II

15 June 1953

Printer: De La Rue
Watermark: Multiple Script CA
Perforation: 13.5 x 13 (£1) ... 12 (others)

49	5c	yellowish-green	.10	.10	.12	.12
a		... corner retouch[1]				
b		... top retouch[2]				
50	10c	orange	.20	.10	.25	.15
51	15c	blue-green	.75	.50	1.00	.60
a		... setting mark				
52	25c	carmine-red	.50	.50	.60	.60
a		... wall flaw (R1/5)	30.00	15.00	40.00	20.00
53	35c	deep ultramarine	1.25	.75	1.50	1.00
54	50c	dull blue	.25	.10	.30	.12
a		... re-entry (R7/1)				
55	70c	brown-grey	.30	.10	.40	.12
a		... setting mark				
56	1/-	sepia & reddish violet	.30	.10	.40	.12
57	2/-	sepia & rose-carmine	.75	.40	1.00	.50
58	5/-	sepia & dull blue	1.40	.75	1.75	1.00
59	10/-	sepia & olive	1.50	7.00	2.00	8.00
60	20/-	chocolate & reddish lilac	4.00	8.00	5.00	10.00
49/60		set of 12	10.00	17.50	12.50	20.00

1954   Royal Visit

27 April 1954

Printer: De La Rue
Watermark: Multiple Script CA
Perforation: 12

61	1/-	sepia & reddish violet	1.10	1.10	1.40	1.40

---

1   Recutting of lines at top right corner (R1/8).
2   Recutting of lines at top and top right (R5/8).

49 62

50 63 51 64

52 65

53 66 54 67

55 68 57 71

56 69

 70  58  72  59  73

 60  74

1954–62 Definitives – Queen Elizabeth II

Printer: Waterlow & Sons; De La Rue after 5 December 1961
Watermark: Multiple Script CA
Perforation: 13.5 x 13 (£1) … 12 x 13½ (35c, 1/25, 2/-, 5/-) … 12 (others)

62	5c	bluish green	1 Jun 55	1.50	2.75	1.75	3.50
a		… corner retouch[3]					
b		… top retouch[4]					
c		… perf 12 x 13.5	12 Apr 56	.20	1.00	.25	1.25
ca		… … corner retouch[3]					
cb		… … top retouch[4]					
63	10c	vermilion	1 Feb 55	.75	.25	1.00	.30
64	15c	greenish grey	26 Apr 59	4.75	5.25	6.00	6.50
a		… setting mark					
b		… deep greenish grey	16 Jan 62	10.00	12.00	12.50	15.00
ba		… … setting mark					
c		… greenish slate	13 Nov 62	14.00	9.50	17.50	12.00
ca		… … setting mark					
65	25c	deep rose red	15 Mar 56	3.25	1.75	4.25	2.00
a		… rose-red	13 Mar 62	10.00	12.00	12.50	15.00
66	35c	deep blue	15 Oct 58	3.25	4.50	4.25	5.50
b		… violet-blue	17 Feb 59	7.50	2.00	9.00	2.50
67	50c	deep blue	1 Jul 55	2.00	1.75	2.50	2.25
a		… re-entry (R7/1)					
b		… perf 12 x 13.5	12 Apr 56	.60	.10	.75	.12
ba		… … re-entry (R7/1)					
bb		… … watermark inverted		–	£500	–	$625
c		… deeper blue	5 Dec 61	.70	.15	1.00	.20
ca		… … re-entry (R7/1)					

---

3 5c corner retouch – recutting of lines at top right corner (R1/8).

4 5c top retouch – recutting of lines at top and top right (R5/8).

				£ MNH	£ FU/CTO	$US MNH	$US FU/CTO
68	70c	black	20 Sep 54	.75	1.00	1.00	1.25
a		... setting mark					
b		... perf 12 x 13.5	12 Apr 56	1.00	.20	1.25	.25
69	1/-	black & violet	1 Jul 55	.75	.10	1.00	.12
70	1/25	blue & black	16 Jul 56	7.00	.50	9.00	.60
a		... weak entry (R6/3)[5]					
a		... dull blue & black	16 Jan 62	10.00	12.00	12.50	15.00
ab		... weak entry (R6/3)					
71	2/-	black & carmine-red	1 Mar 56	7.50	.40	9.50	.50
a		... watermark inverted					
b		... black & carmine-rose	22 Jan 63	25.00	10.00	30.00	12.50
72	5/-	black & deep dull blue	11 Apr 56	8.00	1.00	10.00	1.25
a		... black & blue	11 Dec 62	22.50	10.00	28.00	12.50
73	10/-	black & bronze-green	20 Sep 54	8.00	1.50	10.00	1.75
74	20/-	black & deep lilac	7 Jan 57	30.00	18.00	38.00	22.00
a		... deep black & deep lilac	14 May 58	45.00	15.00	55.00	20.00
62/74		set of 13		65.00	30.00	80.00	37.50
49/60; 62/74		set of 25		75.00	45.00	95.00	55.00

Varieties on Queen Elizabeth II Definitives

(see also footnotes for 5c and 1/25 value varieties.)

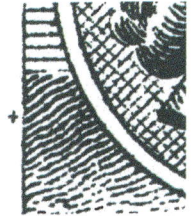

15c – Crater
Setting mark at left side margin.
See 51a, 64a, 64ba, 64ca, 75a, 80b

25c – Mosque
Crack in wall.
See 52a

50c - Map
V-shaped re-entry in Arabic character.
See 54a, 67a, 67ba, 67ca, 83a, 83ba

70c – Salt Works
Setting mark at top margin.
See 55a, 68a

---

5   1/25 weak entry – faint cross-hatching top-left with some diagonal lines missing (R6/3).

					£ MNH	£ FU/CTO	$US MNH	$US FU/CTO

1959   Revised Constitution

26 January 1959

Printer: De La Rue (stamps); Waterlow & Sons (overprints)
Watermark: Multiple Script CA
Perforation: 12

					£ MNH	£ FU/CTO	$US MNH	$US FU/CTO
75		15c	slate green		.75	2.50	1.00	3.00
a			... setting mark					
76		1/25	blue & black		1.10	1.50	1.40	2.00
75/76			set of 2		1.75	4.00	2.20	5.00

75   76

1963   Freedom From Hunger

4 June 1963

Printer: Harrison & Sons
Watermark: Multiple St. Edwards Crown Block CA
Perforation: 14 x 14.5

					£ MNH	£ FU/CTO	$US MNH	$US FU/CTO
77		1/25	bluish green		1.00	2.00	1.25	2.50

77

1964   Definitives – Queen Elizabeth II

5 February 1964

Printer: De La Rue
Watermark: Multiple St. Edwards Crown Block CA
Perforation: 12 (i), 12 x 13.5 (ii)

Stamp designs are identical to the 1953 series.

					£ MNH	£ FU/CTO	$US MNH	$US FU/CTO
78		5c	green (ii)	16 Feb 65	3.50	9.00	4.50	11.00
79		10c	bright orange (i)		1.75	1.00	2.20	1.25

				£ MNH	£ FU/CTO	$US MNH	$US FU/CTO
80	15c	greenish grey (i)		.75	5.00	1.00	6.00
a		… watermark inverted		80.00		$100	
b		… setting mark					
81	25c	bright carmine-red (i)		2.25	.40	2.80	.50
82	35c	indigo-violet (ii)		5.75	4.50	7.25	5.50
83	50c	indigo-blue (ii)		1.00	1.25	1.25	1.50
a		… re-entry (R7/1)					
b		… pale indigo-blue	16 Feb 65				
ba		… … re-entry (R7/1)					
bb		… … watermark inverted					
84	70c	black (ii)		2.25	3.75	2.75	4.50
a		… brownish-grey	16 Feb 65	4.25	9.25	5.25	11.50
85	1/-	black & violet (i)	10 Mar 64	8.75	2.75	11.00	3.50
86	1/25	ultramarine & black (ii)	10 Mar 64	13.00	1.75	16.00	2.20
a		… weak entry (R6/3)[6]					
87	2/-	black & carmine-rose (ii)	16 Feb 65	5.50	29.00	7.00	36.00
78/87		set of 10		40.00	50.00	50.00	62.00

◆

---

[6] Faint cross-hatching top-left with some diagonal lines missing (R6/3).

Federation of South Arabia

1963 – 1967

1 – 2	Nov 1963	Red Cross Centenary
3 – 16	Apr 1965	Definitives
17 – 18	Oct 1965	International Co-operation Year
19 – 22	Jan 1966	Winston Churchill Commemoration
23 – 24	Jul 1966	World Cup Football Championship
25 – 26	Sep 1966	World Health Organsiation HQ Inauguration
27 – 29	Dec 1966	UNESCO 20th Anniversary

1963   Red Cross Centenary

25 November 1963

1	15c	red & black	.35	.35	.45	.45
2	1/25	red & violet-blue	.80	1.40	1.00	1.75
1/2		set of 2	1.15	1.75	1.45	2.20

1

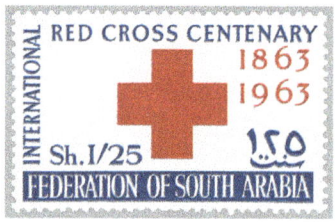
2

1965   Definitives

1 April 1965

3	5f	blue	.10	.05	.12	.07
4	10f	pale violet-blue	.10	.05	.12	.07
5	15f	bluish green	.10	.05	.12	.07
6	20f	green	.10	.05	.12	.07
7	25f	brown-ochre	.10	.05	.12	.07
8	30f	ochre	.10	.05	.12	.07
9	35f	orange-brown	.10	.05	.12	.07
10	50f	red	.10	.05	.12	.07
11	65f	olive-green	.15	.15	.20	.20

				£ MNH	£ FU/CTO	$US MNH	$US FU/CTO
	12	75f	brown-carmine	.15	.05	.20	.07
	13	100f	multicoloured	.25	.05	.30	.07
	14	250f	multicoloured	2.40	.90	3.00	1.10
	15	500f	multicoloured	4.30	.90	5.40	1.10
	16	1D	multicoloured	7.75	11.25	9.75	14.00
3/16			set of 14	14.00	12.50	17.50	15.50

3   4   5   6   7

8   9   10   11   12

 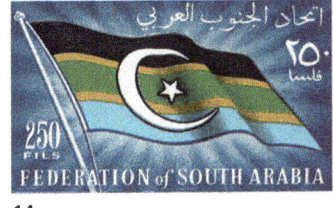 
13   14   15

16

1965   International Co-operation Year

24 October 1965

	17	5f	blue-green & brownish lilac	.25	.30	.30	.40
	18	65f	pale blue & dark green-blue	.90	.85	1.15	1.05
17/18			set of 2	1.15	1.15	1.45	1.45

17   19   20

18   21   22

1966 — Winston Churchill Commemoration
24 January 1966

19	5f	black, gold, cerise & blue	.10	.10	.12	.12
20	10f	black, gold, cerise & deep green	.30	.10	.40	.12
21	65f	black, gold, cerise & purple-brown	.70	.20	.90	.25
22	125f	black, gold, cerise & bluish violet	.95	1.60	1.20	2.00
19/22		set of 4	1.75	1.75	2.20	2.20

1966 — World Cup Football Championship
1 July 1966

23	10f	violet, yellow-green, lake & brown	.60	.50	.75	.65
24	50f	chocolate, blue-green, lake & brown	1.40	1.50	1.75	1.90
23/24		set of 2	2.00	2.00	2.50	2.50

23   24

			£ MNH	£ FU/CTO	$US MNH	$US FU/CTO

1966   World Health Organisation HQ Inauguration

20 September 1966

			£ MNH	£ FU/CTO	$US MNH	$US FU/CTO
25	10f	black, yellow-green & light blue	.40	.10	.50	.12
26	75f	black, light purple & yellow-brown	1.00	.50	1.25	.65
25/26		set of 2	1.40	.60	1.75	.75

25   26

1966   UNESCO 20th Anniversary

15 December 1966

			£ MNH	£ FU/CTO	$US MNH	$US FU/CTO
27	10f	Education	.15	.07	.20	.10
28	65f	Science	.65	.55	.80	.70
29	125f	Culture	1.75	1.90	2.20	2.40
27/29		set of 3	2.25	2.25	2.80	2.80

27   28   29

Kathiri State

1942 – 1968

Kathiri State of Seiyun

1 – 11	1942	Definitives – Sultan Ja'far ibn al-Mansur al-Kathir
12 – 13	1946	Victory
14 – 15	1949	Silver Wedding
16 – 19	1949	75th Anniversary of UPU
20 – 27	1951	Definitives – New Currency
28	1953	Coronation of Queen Elizabeth II
29 – 38	1954	Definitives – Sultan al-Husayn ibn 'Ali al-Kathir
39 – 41	1964	Definitives – Additional Values
42 – 54	1966	Definitives – New Currency (1)
55 – 67	1966	Definitives – New Currency (2)
68 – 76	1966	Olympic Games Host Cities
77 – 84	1966	World Cup Football Championship
85 – 94	1966	ITU Centenary
95 – 103	1966	Paintings – Sir Winston Churchill
104 – 113	1967	World Peace
114 – 124	1967	Paintings
125 – 130	1967	American Astronauts
131 – 132	1967	Sir Winston Churchill Memorial
133	1967	Flora and Fauna
134 – 142	1967	Paintings – Pierre-Auguste Renoir
143 – 150	1967	Winter Olympics – Grenoble, France
151 – 152	1967	12th World Scout Jamboree – Idaho, USA
153 – 161	1967	Paintings – Henri Toulouse-Lautrec
162 – 169	1967	Spanish Riding School – Vienna, Austria
170 – 173	1967	Paintings – Japanese Artists
174 – 175	1967	Summer Olympics – Mexico City (1)
176 – 179	1967	Paintings – Johannes (Jan) Vermeer

Kathiri State in Hadhramaut

180 – 187	1967	John F. Kennedy and Space Program
188 – 189	1967	John F. Kennedy and Abraham Lincoln
190 – 191	1967	Expo 67 – Montreal, Canada
192 – 200	1967	Summer Olympics – Mexico City (2)
201 – 211	1967	Paintings – Sandro Botticelli
212 – 220	1967	Paintings – Edgar Degas
221 – 229	1968	Paintings – Vincent van Gogh
230 – 240	1968	Paintings – German Artists
241 – 244	1968	Arabic Art
245 – 248	1968	Paintings – Horses

				£ MNH	£ FU/CTO	$US MNH	$US FU/CTO

1942 Definitives – Sultan Ja'far ibn al-Mansur al-Kathir
Jul-Oct 1942

Printer: De La Rue
Watermark: Multiple Script CA
Perforations: 14 (½A – 1A), 12 x 13 (other values vertical designs), 13 x 12 (other values horizontal designs)

#	Value	Description	Date	£ MNH	£ FU/CTO	$US MNH	$US FU/CTO
1	½A	blue-green		.15	1.25	.20	1.60
a		… green	8 Mar 48				
2	¾A	brown		.40	2.50	.50	3.10
3	1A	blue		.50	1.25	.65	1.60
4	1½A	deep carmine		.50	1.50	.65	1.90
a		… carmine	8 Mar 48				
5	2A	sepia		.30	1.50	.40	1.90
a		… sepia-brown	8 Mar 48				
6	2½A	blue		.80	1.50	1.00	1.90
7	3A	sepia & carmine		1.25	2.50	1.60	3.00
a		… sepia-brown & carmine	8 Mar 48				
8	8A	red		2.25	.80	2.80	1.00
9	1R	green		5.00	3.00	6.25	3.75
10	2R	blue & purple		10.00	15.00	12.50	18.75
a		… indigo & reddish purple	8 Mar 48				

1

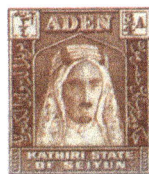
2

3

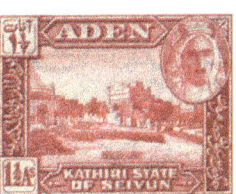
4

5

6

7

8

9

11

10

				£ MNH	£ FU/CTO	$US MNH	$US FU/CTO
11	5R	brown & green	1 Oct 42	25.00	20.00	30.00	25.00
1/11		set of 11		40.00	45.00	50.00	56.00
S		... perforated SPECIMEN		£300	–	$375	–

1946 Victory

15 October 1946

Printer: De La Rue
Watermark: Multiple Script CA
Perforations: 13 x 12 (1½A); 12 x 13 (2½A)

			£ MNH	£ FU/CTO	$US MNH	$US FU/CTO
12	1½A	carmine	.55	.30	.70	.40
13	2½A	blue	.55	.30	.70	.40
a		... overprint inverted	£450		$600	
b		... overprint double	£625		$775	
12/13		set of 2	1.10	.60	1.40	.75
S		... perforated SPECIMEN	£100	–	$125	–

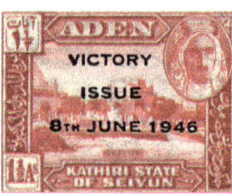

12 13 13a – overprint inverted

1949 Silver Wedding

17 January 1949

Printer: Waterlow & Sons
Watermark: Multiple Script CA
Perforations: 14 x 15 (1½A); 11½ x 11 (5R)

			£ MNH	£ FU/CTO	$US MNH	$US FU/CTO
14	1½A	scarlet	.50	.50	.65	.65
15	5R	green	11.50	11.50	14.50	14.50
14/15		set of 2	12.00	12.00	15.00	15.00

14 15

			£ MNH	£ FU/CTO	$US MNH	$US FU/CTO

1949 — 75th Anniversary of UPU

10 October 1949

Printer: Waterlow & Sons
Watermark: Multiple Script CA
Perforation: 13.7 – 13.9 (2½A, 1R); 11 x 11.5 (3A, 8A)
The 2½A and 1R values' vertical perforation exists in two slightly different measurements, 13.7 and 13.9

No.	Value	Colour	MNH £	FU/CTO £	MNH $US	FU/CTO $US
16	2½A on 20c	ultramarine	.25	.15	.30	.20
17	3A on 30c	carmine-red	2.00	1.50	2.50	1.90
18	8A on 50c	orange	.40	.30	.50	.40
19	1R on 1/-	blue	.50	.35	.65	.45
16/19		set of 4	3.00	2.00	3.75	2.50

16

17

18

19

1951 — Definitives – New Currency

1 October 1951

Printer: Waterlow & Sons
Watermark: Multiple Script CA
Perforation: 14 (5c on 1A), 12 x 13 (other values vertical designs),
13 x 12 (other values horizontal designs)

No.	Value	Colour	MNH £	FU/CTO £	MNH $US	FU/CTO $US
20	5c on 1A	deep blue	.10	1.40	.12	1.75
21	10c on 2A	sepia	.20	1.00	.25	1.25
a		... sepia-brown				
22	15c on 2½A	deep blue	.10	1.50	.12	1.90
23	20c on 3A	sepia & carmine	.10	1.75	.12	2.20
a		... sepia-brown & deep carmine				
24	50c on 8A	vermilion-red	.60	1.10	.75	1.40
25	1/- on 1R	green	1.75	2.50	2.20	3.10

				£ MNH	£ FU/CTO	$US MNH	$US FU/CTO
26	2/- on 2R	indigo & reddish purple		8.50	23.00	10.50	28.00
a		... dark blue & deep purple					
27	5/- on 5R	brown & green		22.50	35.00	28.00	44.00
20/27		set of 8		30.00	60.00	38.00	75.00

20

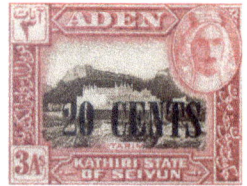 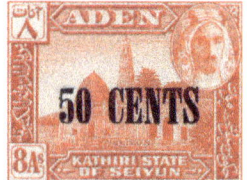 

23   24   26

 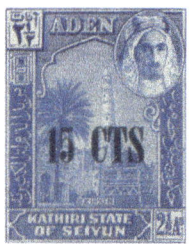   

21   22   25   27   28

1951   Coronation of Queen Elizabeth II

2 June 1953

Printer: De La Rue
Watermark: Multiple Script CA
Perforation: 13½ x 13

28	15c	black & deep green	.90	1.20	1.10	1.50

1954   Definitives – Sultan al-Husayn ibn 'Ali al-Kathir

15 January 1954

Printer: De La Rue
Watermark: Multiple Script CA
Perforation: 12.5 (5c & 10c); others, 12 x 13 (vertical), 13 x 12 (horizontal)

29	5c	sepia	.10	.20	.12	.25
30	10c	deep blue	.10	.20	.12	.25
31	15c	deep bluish-green	.15	.20	.20	.25

29

30

31

32

33

34

35

36

38

37

32	25c	carmine-red		.15	.20	.20	.25
33	35c	deep blue		.15	.20	.20	.25
34	50c	deep brown & carmine-red		.15	.15	.20	.20
35	1/-	brown-orange		.15	.15	.20	.20
36	2/-	deep yellow-green		3.50	2.25	4.50	2.80
37	5/-	deep blue & violet		7.50	9.50	9.50	12.00
38	10/-	yellow-brown & violet		8.00	9.50	10.00	12.00
29/38		set of 10		17.50	20.00	22.00	25.00

1964   Definitives – Additional Values

1 July 1964

Printer: De La Rue
Watermark: Multiple Script CA
Perforation: 12 x 13 (70c), 13 x 12 (others)

39	70c	black		3.00	1.75	3.75	2.20
40	1/25	blue-green		3.00	8.00	3.75	10.00
41	1/50	deep reddish-violet		3.00	8.00	3.75	10.00
39/41		set of 3		8.50	16.00	11.00	20.00

39

40   39   41

1966   Definitives – New Currency (1)

1 April 1966

Watermark: Multiple Script CA
Perforation: 12.5 (5f); others, 12 x 13 (vertical), 13 x 12 (horizontal)

1954/64 series overprinted in red or black as indicated.

42	5f on 5c	black		.20	.15	.25	.20
a		... multiple overprint, one inverted		60.00			
43	5f on 10c	red		.20	1.00	.25	1.25
44	10c on 15c	red		.20	1.40	.25	1.75
a		... overprint inverted		£100		$100	
45	15f on 25c	black		.90	.75	1.10	.95
a		... watermark inverted		60.00		75.00	
46	20f on 35c	red		.30	1.00	.40	1.25
47	25f on 50c	red		.90	1.00	1.10	1.25
48	35f on 70c	red		1.10	1.75	1.40	2.20
49	50f on 1/-	black		.40	.40	.50	.50
50	65f on 1/25	black		.40	.15	.50	.20
51	75f on 1/50	black		1.25	.20	1.60	.25
52	100f on 2/-	red		30.00	38.00	37.50	48.00
53	250f on 5/-	red		1.75	2.75	2.20	3.50
54	500f on 10/-	black		1.75	2.75	2.20	3.50
42/54		set of 13		35.00	45.00	44.00	56.00

1966   Definitives – New Currency (2)

13 August 1966

Watermark: Multiple Script CA
Perforation: 12.5 (5f); others, 12 x 13 (vertical), 13 x 12 (horizontal)

1954/64 series overprinted with deeper spacing and different typeface in colours indicated.

Collectors should be aware that overprint errors on stamps of this set are sometimes incorrectly attributed to the first set issued in April.

55	5f on 5c	blue		1.10	.25	1.40	.30
a		... overprint inverted		55.00		70.00	
b		... overprint in black		25.00		30.00	
c		... overprint in red					

			£ MNH	£ FU/CTO	$US MNH	$US FU/CTO
56	5f on 10c	red	1.40	.25	1.75	.30
57	10f on 15c	yellow	1.40	1.25	1.75	1.60
a		... overprint inverted	40.00		50.00	
58	15f on 25c	blue	1.40	.30	1.75	.40
a		... overprint inverted	45.00		55.00	
59	20f on 35c	yellow	1.40	.30	1.75	.40
60	25f on 50c	blue	1.40	.30	1.75	.40
61	35f on 70c	brown	1.50	.50	1.90	.65
62	50f on 1/-	green	1.75	1.25	2.20	1.60
a		... stop after FILS	20.00		25.00	
63	65f on 1/25	yellow	2.50	1.00	3.10	1.25
64	75f on 1/50	green	3.25	1.75	4.00	2.20
a		... overprint inverted	45.00		55.00	
65	100f on 2/-	yellow	3.75	1.50	4.75	1.90
a		... overprint inverted	45.00		56.00	
66	250f on 5/-	yellow	3.50	2.50	4.50	3.10
a		... overprint inverted	35.00		44.00	
67	500f on 10/-	green	3.50	5.50	4.50	7.00
55/67		set of 13	25.00	15.00	30.00	19.00

1966 Definitives
New currency
1st release

42
small format

45
vertical format

49
horizontal format

1966 Definitives
New currency
2nd release

55
small format

58
vertical format

62
horizontal format

1966   Olympic Games Host Cities

13 August 1966

Watermark: Multiple Script CA
Perforation: 12 x 13 (vertical), 13 x 12 (horizontal)

Numbers 57, 59 and 61 to 67 overprinted in red with an Olympic host city (as indicated), except 35f on 70c, overprinted INTERNATIONAL COOPERATION THROUGH OLYMPICS.

			£ MNH	£ FU/CTO	$US MNH	$US FU/CTO
68	10f on 15c	LOS ANGELES 1932	.80	1.25	1.00	1.50
a		... overprint in black	2.50		3.10	
b		... city overprint inverted				
69	20f on 35c	BERLIN 1936	1.00	1.30	1.25	1.65
a		... overprint in black	3.00		3.75	
b		... South Arabia/value overprint inverted				
70	35f on 70c	INTERNATIONAL COOPERATION ...	1.00	1.30	1.25	1.65
a		... overprint in black	3.00		3.75	
b		... Olympic overprint inverted	30.00		38.00	
71	50f on 1/-	LONDON 1948	1.25	1.75	1.60	2.20
a		... overprint in black	3.50		4.50	
b		... stop after FILS	10.00		12.50	
72	65f on 1/25	HELSINKI 1952	1.25	1.75	1.60	2.20
a		... overprint in black	3.50		4.50	
73	75f on 1/50	MELBOURNE 1956	1.40	2.75	1.75	3.50
a		... overprint in black	4.00		5.00	
74	100f on 2/-	ROME 1960	1.60	3.00	2.00	3.75
a		... overprint in black	4.75		6.00	
75	250f on 5/-	TOKYO 1964	2.25	6.75	2.80	8.50
a		... overprint in black	6.50		8.00	
b		... South Arabia/value overprint inverted	45.00		56.00	
76	500f on 10/-	MEXICO CITY 1968	2.75	8.00	3.50	10.00
a		... overprint in black	8.00		10.00	
68/76		set of 9	12.00	25.00	15.00	30.00
a		... overprint in black	35.00		44.00	

68

69

70

71

74

72

73

75

76

				£ MNH	£ FU/CTO	$US MNH	$US FU/CTO

1966 World Cup Football Championship

19 September 1966

Watermark: Multiple Script CA
Perforation: 12 x 13 (vertical), 13 x 12 (horizontal)

Numbers 57, 59, 61, 62, 65-67 overprinted in black.

				£ MNH	£ FU/CTO	$US MNH	$US FU/CTO
77	10f on 15c	CHAMPION: ENGLAND		.45	.60	.55	.75
78	20f on 35c	FOOTBALL 1966		.60	.60	.75	.75
79	35f on 70c	FOOTBALL 1966		.75	.60	.95	.75
80	50f on 1/-	CHAMPION: ENGLAND		1.00	.60	1.25	.75
a		... stop after FILS		20.00		25.00	
81	100f on 2/-	FOOTBALL 1966		1.75	1.75	2.20	2.20
82	250f on 5/-	CHAMPION: ENGLAND		4.00	6.00	5.00	7.50
83	500f on 10/-	FOOTBALL 1966		5.00	8.50	6.25	10.50
77/83		set of 7		12.00	17.00	15.00	21.00

Number 68 overprinted in black:

84	10f on 15c	LONDON JULY 1966		40.00		50.00	
a		... overprint in blue					

77 – CHAMPION ENGLAND

79 – FOOTBALL 1966

84 – LONDON JULY 1966

1966 ITU Centenary

25 October 1966

85	5f	black, blackish green & violet .... Telstar satellite
a		... black, blackish green & yellow-ochre
86	10f	black, maroon & bright green .... Relay satellite
a		... black, maroon & dark blue
87	15f	black, Prussian blue & yellow-orange .... Ranger satellite
a		... black, Prussion blue & violet
88	25f	black, blackish green & orange .... Telstar satellite
a		... black, blackish green & dark pink
89	35f	black, maroon & olive-yellow .... Relay satellite
a		... black, maroon & orange
90	50f	black, Prussian blue & orange-brown .... Ranger satellite
a		... black, Prussian blue & olive-yellow
91	65f	black, blackish green & orange-yellow .... Telstar satellite
a		... black, blackish green and carmine-pink

			£ MNH	£ FU/CTO	$US MNH	$US FU/CTO
85/91		set of 7	3.50	4.00	4.50	5.00
a		... imperforate – different colours	3.50		4.50	
92	25f + 35f	miniature sheet	7.50		9.50	
a		... imperforate – different colours	15.00		18.75	
93	75f	black & magenta – Ranger satellite	2.00		2.50	
a		... imperforate – black & orange	4.00		5.00	
94	75f	miniature sheet	10.00		12.50	
a		... imperforate – black & orange	15.00		18.75	

89 – Relay   90 – Ranger   91 – Telstar

From the 1966 ITU Centenary set, most Kathiri State issues were of a large format. Images of these stamps are approximately two-thirds actual size and miniature sheets about half size, unless stated otherwise.

1966   Paintings – Sir Winston Churchill

December 1966
CTO stamps sighted dated 26 December 1966.

95	5f	*Sir Winston at his easel*
96	10f	*Antibes*
97	15f	*Flowers*
98	20f	*Tapestries*
99	25f	*Village, Lake Lugano*
100	35f	*Church, Lake Como*
101	50f	*Flowers at Chartwell*
102	65f	*Sir Winston at his easel*

95/102		set of 8	2.00	2.00	2.50	2.50
a		... imperforate	2.50		3.10	
103	65f	miniature sheet	3.50		4.50	
a		... imperforate	10.00		12.50	

95   96   97   98

 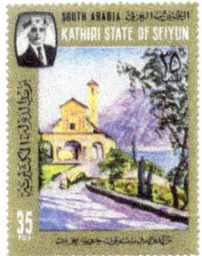  

| 99 | 100 | 101 | 102 |

1967　World Peace

1 January 1967

Watermark: Multiple Script CA
Perforation: 12 x 13 (vertical), 13 x 12 (horizontal)

Numbers 57, 59, 61-67 overprinted in red.

104	10f on 15c	Pandit Nehru
105	20f on 35c	Winston Churchill
106	35f on 70c	Dag Hammarskjold
107	50f on 1/-	John F Kennedy
108	65f on 1/25	Ludwig Erhard
109	75f on 1/50	Lyndon Johnson
110	100f on 2/-	Eleanor Roosevelt
111	250f on 5/-	Winston Churchill
112	500f on 10/-	John F. Kennedy

104/112		set of 9	18.00	23.00
a		... overprint in black	45.00	56.00
107 b	50f on 1/-	... stop after FILS	15.00	19.00
113	65f on 1/25	Johnson-Erhard Meeting	£120	$150

| 104 | 107 | 108 |

| 109 | 111 | 113 |

    105   106   110   112

1967   Paintings

2 February 1967

CTO 5f to 65f stamps sighted dated 16 February 1967.
CTO 75f stamp sighted dated 22 March 1967.

The 75f value is usually marketed as a separate issue.

114	5f	*Master Crewe as Henry VIII*	Joshua Reynolds
115	10f	*The Dancer*	Edgar Degas
116	15f	*The Fifer*	Edouard Manet
117	20f	*Stag At Sharkeys*	George Bellows
118	25f	*Don Manuel Osorio*	Francisco Goya
119	35f	*St. Martin Dividing His Cloak*	Anthony Van Dyke
120	50f	*The Blue Boy*	Thomas Gainsborough
121	65f	*The White Horse*	Paul Gauguin
122	75f	*La Gioconda - Mona Lisa*	Leonardo da Vinci

114/121	5f/65f	set of 8		3.50	2.25	4.50	3.00
a		... imperforate		7.00		8.75	
122	75f	*La Gioconda – Mona Lisa*		1.75	1.75	2.20	1.75
a		... imperforate		2.00		2.50	
123	65f	miniature sheet		5.00		6.25	
a		... imperforate		10.00		12.50	
124	75f	miniature sheet		4.50		5.75	
a		... imperforate		10.00		12.50	

    114   115   116   117

Note: Images of miniature sheets are presented, at approximately half actual size, after the listings.

| 118 | 119 | 120 | 121 | 122 |

1967   American Astronauts

February 1967
Cover sighted dated 15 February 1967.

Perforation: 12 x 13 (vertical), 13 x 12 (horizontal)
Numbers 57, 59, 61, 62, 65 and 66 overprinted in red.

125	10f on 15c	Alan Shepard, Jr
126	20f on 35c	Virgil Grissom
127	25f on 70c	John Glenn, Jr
128	50f on 1/-	Scott Carpenter
129	100f on 2/-	Walter Schirra, Jr
130	250f on 5/-	Gordon Cooper, Jr

125/130		set of 6	5.00	9.00	6.25	11.50
a		... overprint in black	25.00		30.00	
128 b	50f on 1/-	... Stop after FILS	12.00		15.00	
130 b	250f on 5/-	... overprint double	50.00		60.00	

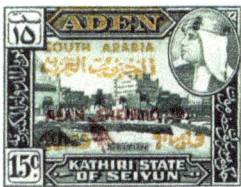  

| 125 | 128 | 130 |

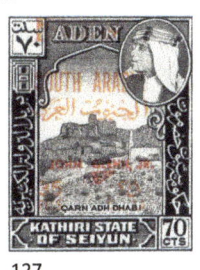 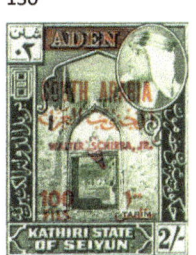

| 126 | 127 | 129 |

1967   Sir Winston Churchill Memorial

March 1967

131	75f	Great Britain Churchill crown	1.00	1.25
a		... imperforate	3.00	3.75

			£ MNH	£ FU/CTO	$US MNH	$US FU/CTO
132	75f	miniature sheet	1.75		2.20	
a		... imperforate	16.00		20.00	

131

1967   Flora and Fauna

			£ MNH	£ FU/CTO	$US MNH	$US FU/CTO
133	20f	bright green & dark violet	.85	.85	1.05	1.05
a		... denomination omitted				
b		... brownish red & dark violet imperforate	.85		1.05	
ba		... ... denomination omitted				

133   133a   133b   133ba

1967   Paintings – Pierre-Auguste Renoir

October 1967
CTO stamps sighted dated 10 October 1967.

134	10f	*The Two Sisters*
135	35f	*Girls at the Piano*
136	50f	*Madame Charpentier with her Children*
137	65f	*In the Garden of Luxembourg*
138	75f	*Jean Renoir Writing*
139	100f	*Young Girl in a Red Hat*
140	200f	*Pink and Blue, Mesdemoiselles Cahen*
141	250f	*Mademoiselle Irene Cahen of Anvers*

			£ MNH	£ FU/CTO	$US MNH	$US FU/CTO
134/141		set of 8	3.00	3.00	3.75	3.75
a		... imperforate	3.00		3.75	
142	250f	miniature sheet	2.25		2.80	
a		... imperforate	8.50		10.50	

134   135   136   137

138   139   140   141

1967   Winter Olympics – Grenoble, France

June 1967
CTO stamps sighted dated 28 August 1967.

143	10f	Speed skating				
144	25f	Ice hockey				
145	35f	Figure skating				
146	50f	Cross country skiing				
147	75f	Downhill skiing				
148	100f	Two-man bobsled				
149	250f	Ski jump				
143/149		set of 7	2.50	2.50	3.10	3.10
a		... imperforate	3.25		4.00	
150	250f	miniature sheet	4.50		5.75	
a		... imperforate	35.00		44.00	

143   144   145

146   147   148   149

				£ MNH	£ FU/CTO	$US MNH	$US FU/CTO

1967   **12th World Scout Jamboree – Idaho, USA**

August 1967
CTO stamps sighted dated 14 August 1967

151	150f	Hunter shooting		.75	.40	.95	0.50
a		... imperforate		2.00		2.50	
152	150f	miniature sheet		1.75		2.20	
a		... imperforate		20.00		25.00	

151

1967   **Paintings – Henri Toulouse-Lautrec**

November 1967
CTO stamps sighted dated 1 November 1967.

153	10f	*The Dance at the Moulin Rouge*
154	35f	*The Clownesse Cha-U-Kao*
155	50f	*Portrait of Aristide Bruant*
156	65f	*At the Circus Fernando, the Rider*
157	75f	*Doctor T. Tapie de Celeyran*
158	100f	*La Goulue Arriving at the Moulin Rouge*
159	200f	*Count Alphonse de Toulouse-Lautrec*
160	250f	*Marcelle Lender Dancing the Bolero in Chilperic*

153/160		set of 8	1.75	1.75	2.20	2.20
a		... imperforate	3.50		4.50	
161	250f	miniature sheet	2.25		2.80	
a		... imperforate	12.50		16.00	

153   154   155   156

Note: Images of miniature sheets are presented, at approximately half actual size, after the listings.

157   158   159   160

1967 Spanish Riding School – Vienna, Austria

November 1967
CTO stamps sighted dated 20 November 1967.

162	10f	Head of a horse				
163	25f	Pas de Deux				
164	35f	Levade				
165	50f	Passage				
166	75f	Courbette				
167	100f	Pas de Deux				
168	250f	Ballotade				
162/168		set of 7	2.25	1.75	2.80	2.20
a		… imperforate	2.00		2.50	
169	250f	miniature sheet	1.75		2.20	
a		… imperforate	12.00		15.00	

162   163   164

165   166   167   168

				£ MNH	£ FU/CTO	$US MNH	$US FU/CTO

1967   Paintings – Japanese Artists

December 1967
CTO stamps sighted dated 28 December 1967.

170	25f	*Self-portrait with his Teacher M. Chosun* … … … … Katsukawa Shunsho
171	150f	*Boats Sailing Home to Yabase* … … … … … … … unknown artist
172	500f	*Young Girl Visiting the Sanctuary* … … … … … … Suzuki Harunobu

			£ MNH	£ FU/CTO	$US MNH	$US FU/CTO
170/172		set of 3	1.75	1.40	2.20	1.75
a		… imperforate	1.75		2.20	
173	500f	miniature sheet	1.75		2.20	
a		… imperforate	20.00		25.00	

 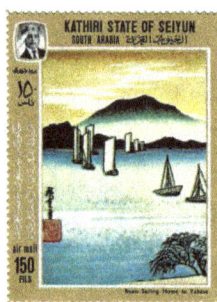 

    170   171   172

1967   Summer Olympics – Mexico City (1)

November 1967

			£ MNH	£ FU/CTO	$US MNH	$US FU/CTO
174	500f	Olympic torch and runner	1.00	1.00	1.25	1.25
a		… imperforate	2.00		2.50	
175	500f	miniature sheet	4.00		5.00	
a		… imperforate	15.00		19.00	

174

1967   Paintings – Johannes (Jan) Vermeer

December 1967
CTO stamps sighted dated 22 January 1968.

176	25f	*The Guitar Player*
177	150f	*Girl with a Pearl Earring*
178	500f	*The Wine Glass*

			£ MNH	£ FU/CTO	$US MNH	$US FU/CTO
176/178		set of 3	1.75	1.25	2.20	1.60
a		... imperforate	2.00		2.50	
179	500f	miniature sheet	1.75		2.20	
a		... imperforate	12.50		16.00	

  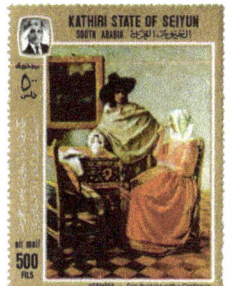

176 177 178

1967 — John F. Kennedy and Space Program

November 1967
CTO stamps sighted dated 14 November 1967.

180	10f	Kennedy, Johnson, von Braun and Saturn I rocket
181	25f	Kennedy inspecting Cape Canaveral
182	35f	Kennedy with John Glenn
183	50f	Kennedy with the seven original astronauts
184	75f	Kennedy addressing astronauts
185	100f	Kennedy and rocket
186	250f	Wright Brothers' Wright Flyer and Mercury space capsule

180/186		set of 7	1.25	1.50	1.60	1.90
a		... imperforate	2.25		2.80	
187	100f+250f	miniature sheet	1.25		1.60	
a		... imperforate	16.00		20.00	

180 182 183

181 185 186 184

				£ MNH	£ FU/CTO	$US MNH	$US FU/CTO

1967 — John F. Kennedy and Abraham Lincoln

November 1967
CTO stamps sighted dated 23 November 1967.

				£ MNH	£ FU/CTO	$US MNH	$US FU/CTO
188	500f	Portraits		.80	1.15	1.00	1.45
a		... imperforate		1.15		1.45	
189	500f	miniature sheet		1.75		2.20	
a		... imperforate		16.00		20.00	

188   190

1967 — Expo '67 – Montreal, Canada

November 1967
CTO stamps sighted dated 23 November 1967.

				£ MNH	£ FU/CTO	$US MNH	$US FU/CTO
190	150f	USA Pavilion		.80	1.15	1.00	1.45
a		... imperforate		2.25		2.80	
191	150f	miniature sheet		1.75		2.20	
a		... imperforate		16.00		20.00	

1967 — Summer Olympics – Mexico City (2)

January 1968
CTO stamps sighted dated 12 January 1968.

				£ MNH	£ FU/CTO	$US MNH	$US FU/CTO
192	10f	1896 Athens					
193	35f	1932 Los Angeles					
194	50f	1936 Berlin					
195	65f	1948 London					
196	75f	1960 Rome					
197	100f	1964 Tokyo					
198	150f	1968 Mexico City					
199	200f	1972 Munich					
192/199		set of 8		1.75	1.15	2.20	1.45
a		... imperforate		2.25		2.80	
200	150f + 200f	miniature sheet		1.75		2.20	
a		... imperforate		20.00		25.00	

Note: Images of miniature sheets are presented, at approximately half actual size, after the listings

192   193   194   195

196   197   198   199

1967   Paintings – Sandro Botticelli

CTO stamps sighted are undated.

201	15f	*Julien de Medicis*	
202	15f	*Man with a Medal*	
203	25f	*Lorenzo Tornabuoni*	
204	25f	*Giovanna degli Albizzi*	
205	30f	*The Return of Judith*	
206	30f	*Pallas and the Centaur*	
207	100f	*Spring* (detail 1)	
208	100f	*Spring* (detail 2)	
209	500f	*Spring* (detail 1)	
210	500f	*Spring* (detail 2)	

201/208		set of 8 gold frame	1.75	1.75	2.20	2.20
a		… imperforate	2.00	2.00	2.50	2.50
211	500f + 500f	miniature sheet gold frame	2.00	2.00	2.50	2.50
a		… blue-silver frame imperforate	6.00		7.50	

201/202   203/204

205/206

207/208

1967   Paintings – Edgar Degas

CTO stamps sighted are undated.

212	10f	*Portraits at the Bourse*
213	35f	*Miss Lala at the Fernando Circus*
214	50f	*Absinthe*
215	65f	*Degas' Father and Pagans*
216	75f	*The Millinery Shop*
217	200f	*Rose-Adelaide Degas*
218	250f	*The Dancing Class*
219	250f	*The Dancing Class* (larger format)

212/218		set of 7 gold frame	1.75	1.75	2.20	2.20
b		... blue-silver frame	1.75		2.20	
ba		... ... imperforate	1.75		2.20	
220	250f	miniature sheet (no. 219) gold frame	1.75		2.20	
a		... blue-silver frame imperforate	10.00		12.50	

212

213

214

215

216   217   218

				£ MNH	£ FU/CTO	$US MNH	$US FU/CTO

1968   Paintings – Vincent van Gogh

CTO stamps sighted off-cover are undated.
Stamps sighted on maximum cards are dated 2 December 1968.

221	10f	*Portrait of Dr Gachet*					
222	35f	*Lieutenant Milliet*					
223	50f	*Young Male Peasant*					
224	65f	*The Letter Carrier*					
225	75f	*La Mousme*					
226	200f	*Schoolboy*					
227	250f	*Madame Ginoux*					
228	250f	*Madame Ginoux* (larger format)					
221/227		set of 7 gold frame		2.75	2.75	3.50	3.50
b		... blue-silver frame		2.75		3.50	
ba		... ... imperforate		6.00		7.50	
229	250f	miniature sheet (no. 228) gold frame		3.50	3.50	4.50	4.50
b		... blue-silver frame imperforate		9.00		11.00	

221   222   223

224   225   226   227

1968   Paintings – German Artists

CTO stamps sighted are undated.

230	15f	*Jean de Dinteville* .... Hans Holbein
231	15f	*Georges de Selve* .... Hans Holbein
232	25f	*Portrait of a Man* .... Hans Baldung
233	25f	*Vanitas* .... Hans Baldung
234	30f	*Elector of Saxony* .... Lucas Cranach
235	30f	*Christiane Eulemann* .... Lucas Cranach
236	100f	*Portrait of Bernhart von Reesen* ... Albrecht Dürer
237	100f	*Portrait of a Venetian* .... Albrecht Dürer

				£ MNH	£ FU/CTO	$US MNH	$US FU/CTO
238		500f	*Portrait of Bernhart von Reesen ....Albrecht Dürer*				
239		500f	*Portrait of a Venetian . . . . .Albrecht Dürer*				
230/237			set of 8 gold frame	1.75	1.75	2.20	2.20
	a		... imperforate	1.75		2.20	
	b		... silver frame	1.75		2.20	
	ba		... ... imperforate	1.75		2.20	
240		500f + 500f	miniature sheet gold frame	2.00		2.50	
	a		... silver frame imperforate	10.00		12.50	

230/231

232/233

234/235

236/237

1968   Arabic Art

CTO stamps sighted dated 23 January 1968.

241		25f	Gold vase				
242		250f	Gold lion				
243		500f	Gold winged horse				
241/243			set of 3	2.25	3.50	2.80	4.50
	a		... imperforate	3.50		4.50	
244		500f	miniature sheet	5.50	5.50	7.00	
	a		... imperforate	10.00		12.50	

Note: Images of miniature sheets are presented, at approximately half actual size, after the listings.

241   242   243

1968   Paintings – Horses

CTO stamps sighted dated November 1967.

Despite this issue being inscribed 'of Seiyun' rather than 'in Hadhramaut' it is usually regarded as the final Kathiri release.

245	150f	*Napoleon Crossing the Alps* – Jacques Louis David	1.10	3.50	1.40	4.50
a		… imperforate	2.25		2.80	
246	150f	miniature sheet	3.50	5.50	4.50	
a		… imperforate	10.00		12.50	
247	500f	*St George and the Dragon* – Rogier van der Weyden	1.25	1.25	1.60	1.60
a		… imperforate	2.50		3.10	
248	500f	miniature sheet	2.25		2.80	
a		… imperforate	10.00		12.50	

245   247

---

30 November 1967

Kathiri State became part of the People's Republic of Southern Yemen on 30 November 1967. The postal validity of all 1968 stamps is therefore in question. Given the lack of known 'issue' dates, some of the later 1967 stamps are also in doubt.

◆

Kathiri State

Miniature Sheets

92 – ITU Centenary

94a – ITU Centenary

103 – Paintings – Sir Winston Churchill

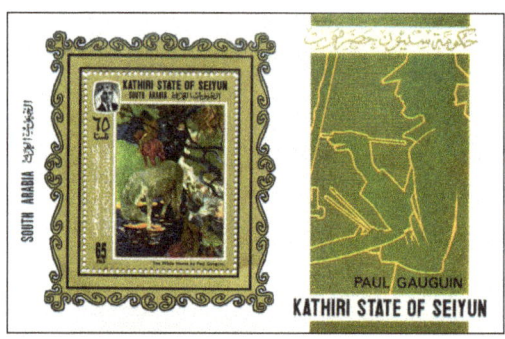
123 – Paintings

124a – Paintings

132 – Sir Winston Churchill Memorial

142 – Paintings – Auguste Renoir

150 – Winter Olympics, Grenoble

152 – 12th World Scout Jamboree, Idaho

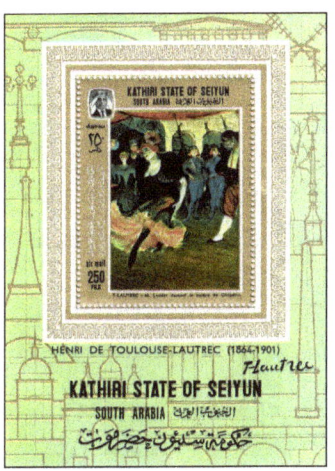
161 – Paintings – Toulouse-Lautrec

169 – Spanish Riding School, Vienna

173 – Paintings – Japanese Artists

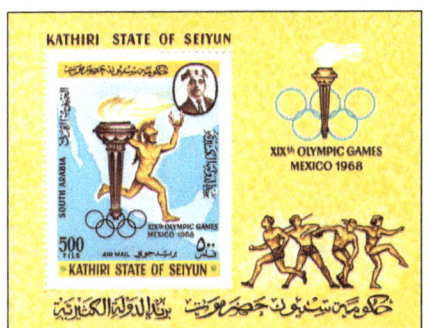
175 – Summer Olympics, Mexico City (1)

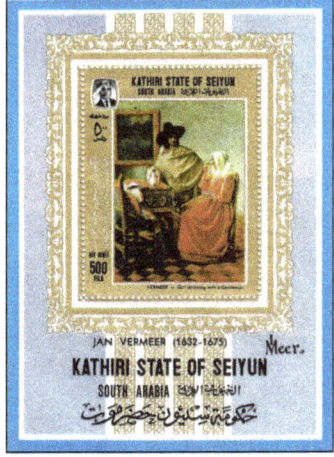
179 – Paintings – Jan Vermeer

187 – Kennedy and Space Program

189 – Kennedy and Lincoln

191 – Expo '67, Montreal

200 – Summer Olympics, Mexico City (2)

211a – Paintings, Sandro Botticelli

220a – Paintings, Edgar Degas

229 – Paintings, Vincent Van Gogh

240 – Paintings, German Artists

244 – Arabic Art

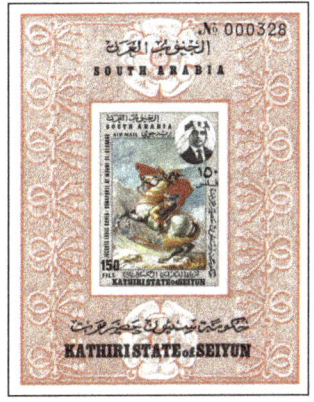

246a
Painting, Napoleon Crossing the Alps

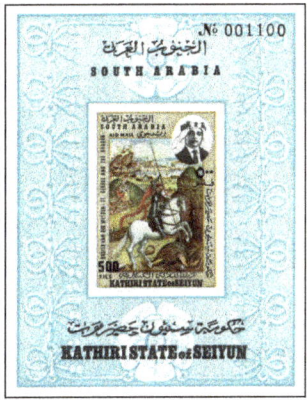

248a
Painting, St George Slaying the Dragon

Mahra State

1967 – 1968

Mahra State of Qishn and Socotra

1 – 11	1967	Definitives
12 – 21	1967	President John F. Kennedy Commemoration
22 – 25	1967	12th World Scout Jamboree – Idaho, USA
26 – 31	1967	Summer Olympics – Mexico City
32 – 41	1967	Arabian Art
42 – 51	1967	Winter Olympics – Grenoble, France
52 – 61	1967	Space Exploration
62 – 72	1967	Paintings
73 – 81	1968	Paintings – Claude Monet
82 – 90	1968	Paintings – Japanese Artists
91 – 99	1968	Paintings – Tiziano Vecelli (Titian)
100 – 108	1968	Paintings – Diego Velázquez
109 – 117	1968	Olympic Gold Medal Winners – France
118 – 126	1968	Olympic Gold Medal Winners – Germany
127 – 135	1968	Olympic Gold Medal Winners – Italy
136 – 144	1968	Olympic Gold Medal Winners – USA
145 – 153	1968	1968 Winter Olympics Gold Medallists – France
154 – 162	1968	1968 Winter Olympics Gold Medallists – Germany
163 – 171	1968	1968 Winter Olympics Gold Medallists – Italy
172 – 180	1968	1968 Winter Olympics Gold Medallists – USA

1967 Definitives

12 March 1967

Flag in green, black and vermilion; inscriptions in black; background colours as indicated.

1	5f	mauve
2	10f	buff
3	15f	sage-green
4	20f	salmon
5	25f	ochre
6	35f	green
7	50f	blue
8	65f	blackish brown
9	100f	violet
10	250f	rose-red
11	500f	grey-green

1/11		set of 11	5.25	3.00	6.50	3.75

3

1967   President John F. Kennedy Commemoration

CTO stamps sighted dated 18 August 1967.

12	10f	President Kennedy	
13	15f	Kennedy receiving medal	
14	25f	John and Jacqueline Kennedy sailing	
15	50f	Wedding of John and Jacqueline Kennedy	
16	75f	Christening of Kennedy's baby	
17	100f	Kennedy meeting people	
18	150f	Kennedy with Lyndon Johnson and Robert Kennedy	
19	250f	Kennedy with John Glenn	
20	500f	Kennedy in the Oval Office	

12/20		set of 9	1.00	1.00	1.25	1.25
a		... imperforate	2.00		2.50	
21	500f	miniature sheet	1.75		2.20	
a		... imperforate	15.00		19.00	

12   13   14   15   16

17   18   19   20

1967   12th World Scout Jamboree – Idaho , USA

1 September 1967
CTO stamps sighted dated 11 October 1967.

22	15f	Scout emblem and map of North America
23	75f	Scout and tents

				£ MNH	£ FU/CTO	$US MNH	$US FU/CTO
24		100f	Field exercise				
25		150f	Scouts from various nations				
22/25			set of 4	1.25	1.25	1.60	1.60
a			... imperforate	2.50		3.10	

22 23 24 25

1967 — Summer Olympics – Mexico City

				£ MNH	£ FU/CTO	$US MNH	$US FU/CTO
26		10f	Discus throwing				
27		25f	Basketball				
28		50f	Gymnastics				
29		250f	Running				
30		500f	Fencing				
26/30			set of 5	2.50	2.50	3.10	3.10
a			... imperforate	2.50		3.10	
31		500f	miniature sheet	2.50		3.10	
a			... imperforate	15.00		19.00	

26 27 28 29 30

1967 — Arabian Art

CTO stamps sighted dated 6 November 1967.
CTO miniature sheet sighted dated 1 November 1967.

32		10f	*Miraculous Saving*
33		15f	*Nishapur pottery*
34		25f	*Odalisques*
35		50f	*Paladin's Veterinarian Artbook*
36		75f	*Young Prince Reading*
37		100f	*Mohammed Riding Animal of the Night*

				£ MNH	£ FU/CTO	$US MNH	$US FU/CTO
38	150f		Two Saints				
39	250f		Portrait of a Miniaturist				
40	500f		History of Bayad				
32/40			set of 9	1.75	1.75	2.20	2.20
a			... imperforate	3.75		4.75	
41	250f + 500f		miniature sheet	6.00		7.50	
a			... imperforate	7.50		9.50	

1967   Winter Olympics – Grenoble, France

CTO stamps sighted dated 14 November 1967.

42	10f	Cross-country skiing					
43	15f	Slalom					
44	25f	Four-man bobsled					
45	50f	Ice hockey					
46	75f	Speed skating					
47	100f	Ice dance					
48	150f	Figure skating					
49	250f	Ski jumping					
50	500f	Biathlon					
42/50		set of 9	2.00	2.00	2.50	2.50	
a		... imperforate	3.50		4.50		
51	250f + 500f	miniature sheet	4.50	4.50	5.75	5.75	
a		... imperforate	20.00		25.00		

42   43   44   45

46   47   48   49   50

1967   Space Exploration

CTO stamps sighted dated 4 December 1967.
CTO miniature sheet sighted dated 11 January 1968.

52	10f	Mercury capsule	
53	15f	Mercury capsule at re-entry	
54	25f	Saturn V rocket	
55	50f	Apollo lunar module	
56	75f	Rocket and capsule	
57	100f	Apollo lunar module	
58	150f	Apollo capsule under parachutes	
59	250f	Multi-stage rocket	
60	500f	Capsule	

52/60		set of 9	1.75	1.75	2.20	2.20
	a	... imperforate	5.00		6.25	
61	250f + 500f	miniature sheet	4.00	4.00	5.00	5.00
	a	... imperforate	15.00		19.00	

52   53   54   55

56   57   58   59   60

> **30 November 1967**
>
> Mahra State became part of the People's Republic of Southern Yemen on 30 November 1967. The postal validity of all 1968 stamps is therefore in question. Given the lack of known 'issue' dates, some of the later 1967 stamps are also in doubt.

1967   Paintings

CTO stamps sighted dated 26 December 1967.
CTO miniature sheet sighted dated 11 January 1968.

62	10f	*Jan Asselyn*	Frans Hals
63	15f	*Black Pigs*	Paul Gauguin
64	25f	*Young Girl Reading*	Jean-Honoré Fragonard
65	50f	*Portrait of Charles V*	Bernard van Orley
66	75f	*Spring* (detail)	Sandro Botticelli
67	100f	*Peasants at the Table*	Diego Velázquez
68	150f	*Portrait of a Married Couple*	Anthony van Dyke
69	250f	*The Fortune Teller*	Michelangelo Merisi da Caravaggio
70	500f	*The Oath of the Horatii* (detail) ...	Jacques Louis David
71	500f	*The Oath of the Horatii* (detail) (different frame)	

62/70		set of 9	1.75	1.75	2.20		2.20
a		... imperforate	2.75		3.50		
72	500f	miniature sheet (no. 71)	3.50		4.50		
a		... imperforate	15.00		19.00		

62   63   64   65   66   70

67   68   69

Note: Images of miniature sheets are presented, at approximately half actual size, after the listings.

				£ MNH	£ FU/CTO	$US MNH	$US FU/CTO
1968		**Paintings – Claude Monet**					
	73	10f	*Saint-Lazare Railway Station, Paris*				
	74	15f	*Terrace near Havre*				
	75	25f	*Hotel des Roches Noires, Trouville*				
	76	50f	*Women in the Garden*				
	77	75f	*Women on the Beach, Trouville*				
	78	100f	*La Grenouillère*				
	79	150f	*Camille Monet with Dog*				
	80	500f	*Camille Monet with Dog*				
73/79			set of 7 bistre-yellow frame	1.00	1.00	1.25	1.25
	a		... imperforate bistre-yellow frame	4.25		5.25	
	b		... imperforate rose-red frame	7.00		8.75	
	81	500f	miniature sheet	5.00		6.25	
	a		... imperforate	20.00		25.00	

73 74 75 76

77 78 79 82a 83a 84a

85a 86a 87a 88a

1968   Paintings – Japanese Artists

					£ MNH	£ FU/CTO	$US MNH	$US FU/CTO
82	10f	Two Women	....	Suzuki Harunobu				
83	15f	Women Working Cotton						
84	25f	Two Women	....	Torii Kiyonaga				
85	50f	Woman	....	Kano Hideyori				
86	75f	Dance	....	Kano Naganobu				
87	100f	Samurai Sword						
88	150f	Picnic Party						
89	500f	Picnic Party						
82/88		set of 7 pink frame			1.75	1.75	2.20	2.20
a		... imperforate pale blue frame			5.00		6.00	
90	500f	miniature sheet pink frame			4.00		5.00	
a		... imperforate pale blue frame			20.00		25.00	

91   92   93   94

95   96   97   100   101   102

103   104   105   106

				£ MNH	£ FU/CTO	$US MNH	$US FU/CTO

1968   Paintings – Tiziano Vecelli (Titian)

91	10f	*Festival of Venus*					
92	15f	*Portrait of Pietro Aretino*					
93	25f	*Portrait of a Venetian Lady*					
94	50f	*Portrait of Ippolito Riminaldi*					
95	75f	*Magdalena*					
96	100f	*Portrait of a Man*					
97	150f	*Sacred and Profane Love*					
98	500f	*Sacred and Profane Love*					
91/97		set of 7 pale blue frame	2.75	2.75	3.50	3.50	
a		... imperforate pink frame	4.50		5.75		
99	500f	miniature sheet pale blue frame	4.50		5.75		
a		... imperforate pink frame	10.00		12.50		

1968   Paintings – Diego Velázquez

Stamps sighted on maximum cards dated 2 December 1968.

100	10f	*The Spinners*					
101	15f	*The Water Carrier*					
102	25f	*Queen Mariana*					
103	50f	*The Triumph of Bacchus*					
104	75f	*Old Woman Cooking Eggs*					
105	100f	*The Infanta Margarita*					
106	150f	*The Infant Margarita Maria*					
107	500f	*The Infant Margarita Maria*					
100/106		set of 7 yellow frame	1.25	1.25	1.60	1.60	
a		... imperforate pink frame	3.50		4.50		
108	500f	miniature sheet yellow frame	3.50		4.50		
a		... imperforate pink frame	10.00		12.50		

109   110   111   112

113   114   115

		£ MNH	£ FU/CTO	$US MNH	$US FU/CTO

1968   Olympic Gold Medal Winners – France

109	10f	Rowing (single sculls)	Hermann Barrelet (1900)
110	15f	Wrestling	Henri Deglane (1924)
111	25f	Weightlifting	Louis Hostin (1936)
112	50f	Downhill Skiing	Henri Oreiller (1948)
113	75f	Swimming	Jean Boiteux (1952)
114	100f	Cycling	Michel Rousseau (1956)
115	150f	Showjumping	Pierre d'Oriola (1964)
116	500f	Downhill Skiing	Henri Oreiller (1948)

109/115		set of 7	2.75	2.75	3.50	3.50
a		… imperforate	4.25		5.25	
117	500f	miniature sheet	4.00		5.00	
a		… imperforate	15.00		19.00	

1968   Olympic Gold Medal Winners – Germany

118	10f	Wrestling	Carl Schumann (1896)
119	15f	Swimming (400m breaststroke)	Walter Bathe (1912)
120	25f	Weightlifting	Josef Straßberger (1928)
121	50f	Javelin	Gerhard Stöck (1936)
122	75f	Boxing	Wolfgang Behrendt (1956)
123	100f	Figure Skating	Manfred Schnelldorfer (1964)
124	150f	Decathlon	Willi Holdorf (1964)
125	500f	Decathlon	Willi Holdorf (1964)

118/124		set of 7	2.75	2.75	3.50	3.50
a		… imperforate	4.25		5.25	
126	500f	miniature sheet	4.00		5.00	
a		… imperforate	15.00		19.00	

118   119   120   121

122   123   124

	£ MNH	£ FU/CTO	$US MNH	$US FU/CTO

1968 **Olympic Gold Medal Winners – Italy**

127	10f	Weightlifting . . . . Giuseppe Tonani (1924)
128	15f	Boxing . . . . Piero Toscani (1928)
129	25f	Cycling . . . . Attilio Pavesi (1932)
130	50f	Fencing . . . . Giulio Gaudini (1936)
131	75f	Discus Throw . . . . Adolfo Consolini (1948)
132	100f	Downhill Skiing . . . . Zeno Colò (1952)
133	150f	Shooting . . . . Galliano Rossini (1956)
134	500f	Shooting . . . . Galliano Rossini (1956)

			£ MNH	£ FU/CTO	$US MNH	$US FU/CTO
127/133		set of 7	2.75	2.75	3.50	3.50
a		… imperforate	4.25		5.25	
135	500f	miniature sheet	4.00		5.00	
a		… imperforate	15.00		19.00	

1968 **Olympic Gold Medal Winners – USA**

136	10f	Wrestling . . . . Bernhoff Hansen (1904)
137	15f	Javelin . . . . Mildred "Babe" Didsrikson (1932)
138	25f	Running . . . . James "Jesse" Owens (1936)
139	50f	Shooting . . . . Huelet "Joe" Benner (1952)
140	75f	Weightlifting . . . . Paul Anderson (1956)
141	100f	Boxing . . . . Cassius Clay (1960)
142	150f	Swimming . . . . Donald Schollander (1964)
143	500f	Swimming . . . . Donald Schollander (1964)

			£ MNH	£ FU/CTO	$US MNH	$US FU/CTO
136/142		set of 7	2.75	2.75	3.50	3.50
a		… imperforate	4.25		5.25	
144	500f	miniature sheet	4.00		5.00	
a		… imperforate	15.00		19.00	

    136   137   138   139

 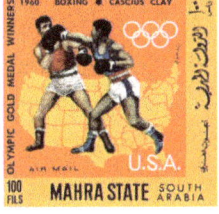 

    140   141   142

1968   1968 Winter Olympics Gold Medallists – France

Numbers 109 to 117 (Gold Medal Winners – France) overprinted.

145/151		set of 7	4.00	5.00
a		... imperforate		
153	500f	miniature sheet	4.00	5.00

WINNER GRENOBLE
1968
JEAN
CLAUDE
KILLY

WINNER GRENOBLE
1968
MARIELLE
GOITSCHEL

          145   148

1968   1968 Winter Olympics Gold Medallists – Germany

Numbers 118 to 126 (Gold Medal Winners – Germany) overprinted.

154/160		set of 7	4.00	5.00
a		... imperforate		
162	500f	miniature sheet	4.00	5.00

Note: Images of miniature sheets are presented, at approximately half actual size, after the listings.

			£ MNH	£ FU/CTO	$US MNH	$US FU/CTO

1968 — 1968 Winter Olympics Gold Medallists – Italy

Numbers 127 to 135 (Gold Medal Winners – Italy) overprinted.

163/169		set of 7	4.00		5.00	
a		... imperforate				
171	500f	miniature sheet	4.00		5.00	

1968 — 1968 Winter Olympics Gold Medallists – USA

Numbers 136 to 144 (Gold Medal Winners – USA) overprinted.

172/178		set of 7	4.00		5.00	
a		... imperforate				
180	500f	miniature sheet	4.00		5.00	

155

WINNER GRENOBLE
1968 • SKATING
ERHARD KELLER

169

GOLD MEDAL
GRENOBLE 1968
NORDIC SKI
FRANCO
NONES

172

GOLD MEDAL
GRENOBLE
1968 • ART SKATING
PEGGY
FLEMING

Mahra State

Miniature Sheets

21 – Kennedy Commemmoration

31 – Summer Olympics, Mexico City

41 – Arabian Art

51 – Winter Olympics, Grenoble

61a – Space Exploration

72 – Paintings

99a – Paintings – Titian

Miniature sheets of Mahra State's Paintings series each follow the same format. The Summer Olympics sets are also styled alike. The Tiziano Vecelli (Titian) and Medal Winners USA sheets are depicted here.

144 – Olympic Gold Medal Winners

Qu'aiti State
1942 – 1968

Qu'aiti State of Shihr and Mukalla

1 –	11	1942	Definitives – Sultan Sir Saleh bin Ghalib al-Qu'aiti
12 –	13	1946	Victory
14 –	15	1948	Silver Wedding
16 –	19	1949	75th Anniversary of UPU
20 –	27	1951	Definitives – New Currency
28		1953	Coronation of Queen Elizabeth II

Qu'aiti State in Hadhramaut

29 –	40	1955	Definitives – Qu'aiti Industries
41 –	52	1963	Definitives – Sultan Ghalib bin Awadh Al-Qu'aiti II
53 –	64	1966	Definitives – New Currency
65 –	67	1966	Winston Churchill Commemoration
68 –	70	1966	President John F. Kennedy Commemoration
71 –	79	1966	World Cup Football Championship
80 –	81	1966	Summer Olympics – Mexico City (1)
82 –	90	1966	International Co-operation Year
91 –	98	1967	STAMPEX – Philatelic Exhibition, London
99 –	100	1967	AMPHILEX – Philatelic Exhibition, Amsterdam
101 –	104	1967	Coronation of Sultan Ghalib bin Awadh al-Qu'aiti II
105 –	106	1967	Summer Olympics – Mexico City (2)
107 –	114	1967	Paintings
115 –	116	1967	12th World Scout Jamboree – Idaho, USA
117 –	125	1967	1968 Winter Olympics – Grenoble, France
126 –	133	1967	Space Exploration
134 –	141	1967	Paintings – Edouard Manet
142 –	143	1967	EXPO 67 – World's Fair, Montreal
144 –	145	1967	36th Monte Carlo Rally
146 –	147	1967	Painting – *Wolf Hunt*, Peter Paul Rubens
148 –	149	1967	Apollo 1 Astronauts Memorial
150 –	155	1967	Paintings – Pierre-Auguste Renoir
156 –	166	1967	Paintings – Lucas Cranach the Elder
167 –	174	1967	Paintings – Equestrian
175 –	178	1967	Paintings – Rembrandt van Rijn
179 –	187	1967	International Tourist Year – Paintings
188 –	203	1968	Prehistoric and Modern Animals
204 –	218	1968	Seven Wonders of the World, Ancient and Modern
219 –	227	1968	Ancient and Modern Olympic Games
228 –	236	1968	Aeroplanes and Space Craft
237 –	238	1968	EFIMEX – Philatelic Exhibition, Mexico City

1942 Definitives – Sultan Sir Saleh bin Ghalib al-Qu'aiti

1 July 1942

Printer: De La Rue
Watermark: Multiple Script CA
Perforations: 14 (i), 13.75 x 14 (ii), 11.75 x 13 (iii)

				£ MNH	£ FU/CTO	$US MNH	$US FU/CTO
1	½A	deep green (i)		.60	.20	.75	.25
a		... olive green (ii)	18 Dec 46				
b		... deep olive-green (ii)	6 Mar 50				
2	¾A	chestnut (i)		.90	.10	1.10	.12
a		... chestnut (ii)					
3	1A	deep blue (i)		.40	.40	.50	.50
a		... blue (ii)					
b		... dark blue (ii)	12 Aug 48				
4	1½A	carmine (iii)		.70	.20	.90	.25
a		... deep carmine (iii)	6 Mar 50				
5	2A	sepia (iii)		.70	.70	.90	.90
a		... yellowish-brown (iii)	18 Dec 46				
b		... sepia-brown (iii)	12 Aug 48				
6	2½A	deep blue (iii)		.20	.10	.25	.12
7	3A	sepia & carmine (iii)		.45	.40	.60	.50
a		... sepia & deep carmine (iii)	6 Mar 50				
8	8A	vermilion-red (iii)		.45	.15	.60	.20

1

2

3

4

5

7

9

6

8

10

11

				£ MNH	£ FU/CTO	$US MNH	$US FU/CTO
9	1R	green (iii)		2.75	2.00	3.50	2.50
a		... A of CA missing from watermark					
10	2R	deep blue & deep purple (iii)	1 Oct 42	7.00	7.00	8.75	8.75
a		... greenish-blue & red-purple (iii) 6 Mar 50					
11	5R	chestnut & green (iii)		14.00	9.00	17.50	11.00
1/11		set of 11		26.00	18.00	31.00	22.50
S		... perforated SPECIMEN		£150		$190	

1946 Victory

15 October 1946

Printer: De La Rue
Watermark: Multiple Script CA
Perforation: 12 x 13 (1½A), 13 x 12 (2½A)

			£ MNH	£ FU/CTO	$US MNH	$US FU/CTO
12	1½A	carmine	.25	.25	.30	.30
13	2½A	blue	.25	.25	.30	.30
12/13		set of 2	.50	.50	.65	.65
S		... perforated SPECIMEN	45.00		55.00	

1949 Silver Wedding

17 January 1949

Printer: Waterlow & Sons
Watermark: Multiple Script CA
Perforation: 14 x 15 (1½A), 11.5 x 11 (5R)

			£ MNH	£ FU/CTO	$US MNH	$US FU/CTO
14	1½A	scarlet	.50	.50	.65	.65
15	5R	green	11.50	11.50	14.50	14.50
14/15		set of 2	12.00	12.00	15.00	15.00

12
VICTORY
ISSUE
8TH JUNE
1946

13
VICTORY
ISSUE
8TH JUNE 1946

14

15

				£ MNH	£ FU/CTO	$US MNH	$US FU/CTO

1949 — 75th Anniversary of UPU

10 October 1949

Watermark: Multiple Script CA
Perforation: 13.7 – 14 (2½A, 1R), 11 x 11.5 (3A, 8A)
The 2½A and 1R values' vertical perforation exists in two slightly different measurements, 13.7 and 13.9

				£ MNH	£ FU/CTO	$US MNH	$US FU/CTO
16	2½A on 20c	ultramarine		.10	.20	.12	.25
17	3A on 30c	carmine-red		.90	.90	1.10	1.10
18	8A on 50c	orange		.15	.90	.20	1.10
19	1R on 1/-	blue		.20	.15	.25	.20
a		... surcharge omitted		£2,900		$3,500	
16/19		set of 4		1.25	2.00	1.60	2.50

16

17

18

19

1951 — Definitives – New Currency

1 October 1951

1942 series overprinted in red (5c) or black (other values).

				£ MNH	£ FU/CTO	$US MNH	$US FU/CTO
20	5c on 1A	deep blue		.05	.10	.07	.12
a		... dark blue					
21	10c on 2A	sepia		.05	.10	.07	.12
a		... yellowish-brown					
b		... sepia-brown					
22	15c on ½A	deep blue		.05	.10	.07	.12
23	20c on 3A	sepia & carmine		.10	.40	.12	.50
a		... sepia & deep carmine					
b		... surcharge double (one albino)					
24	50c on 8A	vermilion-red		.20	1.10	.25	1.40
a		... scarlet red	18 Aug 54				
25	1/- on 1R	green		.90	.20	1.15	.25

				£ MNH	£ FU/CTO	$US MNH	$US FU/CTO
26	2/- on 2R	greenish blue & red-purple		3.50	12.00	4.50	15.00
27	5/- on 5R	chestnut & green		9.50	17.00	11.50	21.00
20/27		set of 8		13.00	28.00	16.00	35.00

20
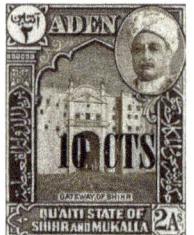
21
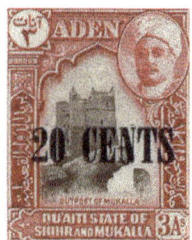
23

25

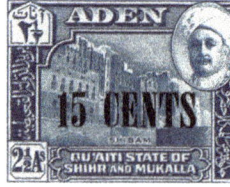
22   24   26   27

1953 Coronation of Queen Elizabeth II
2 June 1953

Printer: De La Rue
Watermark: Multiple Script CA
Perforation: 13.5 x 13

28	15c	black & deep blue	.90	1.20	1.10	1.50

28

1955 Definitives – Qu'aiti Industries
1 September 1955

Printer: De La Rue
Watermark: Multiple Script CA
Perforation: 11.5 x 13–13.5 (vertical format), 14 (horizontal format)

29	5c	greenish blue	.50	.05	.65	.07
30	10c	black	.60	.05	.75	.07
31	15c	dark green	.50	.05	.65	.07
a		... bronze-green	.50	.20	.65	.25

			£ MNH	£ FU/CTO	$US MNH	$US FU/CTO
32	25c	carmine-red	.25	.05	.30	.07
33	35c	ultramarine	.50	.05	.65	.07
34	50c	orange-red	.70	.05	.90	.07
a		... red-orange	.50	.15	.65	.20
35	90c	sepia	.35	.10	.45	.12
36	1/-	black & deep violet	.50	.05	.65	.07
37	1/25	black & red-orange	.35	.30	.45	.40
38	2/-	black & dark blue	2.00	.35	2.50	0.45
39	5/-	black & bluish green	2.50	1.75	3.10	2.20
40	10/-	black & carmine-lake	8.50	4.50	10.50	5.75
29/40		set of 12	14.00	6.50	17.50	8.25

				£ MNH	£ FU/CTO	$US MNH	$US FU/CTO

1963 Definitives – Sultan Ghalib bin Awadh Al-Qu'aiti II

20 October 1963

Printer: De La Rue
Watermark: Multiple Script CA
Perforation: 11.5 x 13-13.5 (vertical format), 14 (horizontal format)
Designs are identical to the 1955 series but with inset portrait of Sultan Awadh II ibn Saleh al-Qu'aiti. The 90c value was changed to 70c.

No.	Value	Colour	£ MNH	£ FU/CTO	$US MNH	$US FU/CTO
41	5c	greenish blue	.05	.75	.07	.95
42	10c	black	.05	.75	.07	.95
43	15c	dark green	.05	.75	.07	.95
44	25c	carmine-red	.10	.35	.12	.45
45	35c	ultramarine	.10	1.00	.12	1.25
46	50c	orange-red	.10	.50	.12	.65
47	70c	sepia	.15	.35	.20	.45
48	1/-	black & deep violet	.15	.15	.20	.20
49	1/25	black & red-orange	.35	3.00	.45	3.75
50	2/-	black & dark blue	2.00	1.50	2.50	1.90
51	5/-	black & bluish green	9.00	15.00	11.00	19.00
52	10/-	black & carmine-lake	19.00	15.00	24.00	19.00
41/52		set of 12	28.00	35.00	35.00	44.00

46   58

1966 Definitives – New Currency

1 April 1966

Designs are identical to the 1963 series but overprinted SOUTH ARABIA and new value, in English and Arabic.

No.	Value	Colour	£ MNH	£ FU/CTO	$US MNH	$US FU/CTO
53	5f on 5c	greenish blue	.10	1.00	.12	1.25
54	5f on 10c	black	1.25	1.50	1.60	1.90
55	10f on 15c	dark green	.10	1.00	.12	1.25
56	15f on 25c	carmine	.10	1.75	.12	2.20
57	20f on 35c	ultramarine	.10	2.75	.12	3.50
58	25f on 50c	orange-red	.10	2.00	.12	2.50
59	35f on 70c	brown	.10	1.50	.12	1.90
60	50f on 1/-	black & deep violet	.50	.25	.65	.30

				£ MNH	£ FU/CTO	$US MNH	$US FU/CTO
	61	65f on 1/25	black & red-orange	1.25	.35	1.60	.45
	62	100f on 2/-	black & dark blue	3.50	1.00	4.50	1.25
	63	250f on 5/-	black & bluish green	1.75	1.25	2.20	1.60
	64	500f on 10/-	black & carmine-lake	22.50	2.75	28.00	3.50
53/64			set of 12	28.00	15.00	35.00	19.00

1966   Winston Churchill Commemoration

1 April 1966

Three values of the 1966 new currency series were overprinted 1874 – 1965 / WINSTON CHURCHILL in red or blue.

				£ MNH	£ FU/CTO	$US MNH	$US FU/CTO
	65	5f on 10c	black (red overprint)	2.75	5.75	3.50	7.25
	a		... black overprint	5.75		7.25	
	66	10f on 15c	dark green (red overprint)	3.25	6.00	4.00	7.50
	a		... black overprint	6.25		7.75	
	b		... red overprint inverted	45.00		56.00	
	67	15f on 25c	carmine (blue overprint)	3.50	6.00	4.50	7.50
	a		... black overprint	7.00		8.75	
65/67			set of 3	8.50	16.00	10.50	20.00
	a		... black overprint	17.00		21.00	

65   66   67   67a

1966   President John F. Kennedy Commemoration

1 April 1966

Three values of the 1966 new currency series were overprinted 1917 – 1963 / JOHN F. KENNEDY in red or blue.

				£ MNH	£ FU/CTO	$US MNH	$US FU/CTO
	68	20f on 35c	ultramarine (red overprint)	1.25	5.00	1.60	6.25
	a		... black overprint	5.75		7.25	
	69	25f on 50c	orange-red (blue overprint)	1.25	5.50	1.60	7.00
	a		... black overprint	5.75		7.25	
	70	35f on 70c	brown (blue overprint)	1.25	6.25	1.60	7.75
	a		... black overprint	5.75		7.25	
68/70			set of 3	3.00	15.00	3.75	19.00
	a		... black overprint	15.00		19.00	

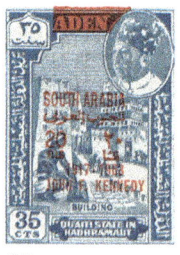   

1917-1963 JOHN F. KENNEDY	68	69	70	69a

1966 World Cup Football Championship

11 August 1966

71	5f	World Cup emblem	
72	10f	Wembley Stadium	
73	15f	Footballers	
74	20f	Jules Rimet Cup and football	
75	25f	World Cup emblem	
76	35f	Wembley Stadium	
77	50f	Footballers	
78	65f	World Cup emblem	

71/78		set of 8	1.75	1.75	2.20	2.20
a		… imperforate	5.00		6.25	
79	50f + 65f	miniature sheet	7.50		9.50	
a		… imperforate	16.50		20.00	

From the 1966 World Cup Football Championship set, Qu'aiti State issues were of a large format. Images are presented at two-thirds actual size and miniature sheets about half size.

				£ MNH	£ FU/CTO	$US MNH	$US FU/CTO

1966   Summer Olympics – Mexico City (1)

25 October 1966

				£ MNH	£ FU/CTO	$US MNH	$US FU/CTO
80	75f	Sombrero and poncho		.85	.85	1.05	1.05
a		... imperforate		1.25		1.60	
81	75f	miniature sheet		2.25		2.80	
a		... imperforate		25.00		30.00	

80

1966   International Co-operation Year

October 1966
CTO stamps sighted dated 8 December 1966.

				£ MNH	£ FU/CTO	$US MNH	$US FU/CTO
82	5f	purple-brown, mauve & green					
a		... imperforate (purple-brown, olive-yellow & green)					
83	10f	blue-violet, orange, green & blue					
a		... imperforate (grey-violet, blue & red)					
84	15f	brown-purple, blue & orange-red					
a		... imperforate (dark green, pink-carmine & blue)					
85	20f	dark blue, deep mauve & orange-red					
a		... imperforate (dark blue, yellowish green & orange-red)					
86	25f	blue-violet, olive-yellow, red and green					
a		... imperforate (dark blue, grey-lilac & carmine)					
b		... red (TOKIO 1964 inscription) omitted[7]					
ba		... red (TOKIO 1964 inscription) omitted[7]					
87	35f	purple-brown, dull vermilion & blue					
a		... imperforate (purple-brown, yellow-olive & orange-red)					
b		... blue (face value) omitted					
88	50f	purple-brown, green & orange-red					
a		... imperforate (dark green, red & blue)					
89	65f	purple-brown, dull violet-blue & orange red					
a		... imperforate (dark blue, red & yellowish green)					
82/89		set of 8		5.00	6.00	6.25	7.50
a		... imperforate (alternate colours)		17.50		22.00	
87 b	35f	... blue (face value) omitted					
90	5f + 25f	miniature sheet		4.50		5.75	
a		... imperforate					

---

7   The 25f stamps with TOKIO 1964 omitted are from the miniature sheets.

82　　　　　　　　83　　　　　　　　84　　　　　　　　85

86　　　　　　　　87　　　　　　　　88　　　　　　　　89

1967　　STAMPEX – Philatelic Exhibition, London

May 1967
CTO stamps sighted dated 2 May 1967.

91	5f	1954 India – head inverted				
92	10f	1901 USA – train inverted				
93	15f	1919 Austria – parliament building inverted				
94	20f	1902 New Zealand – centre inverted				
95	25f	1851 Baden – colour error				
96	50f	1855 Sweden – colour error				
97	65f	1847 Mauritius – 2d "POST OFFICE" error				
91/97		set of 7	1.75	1.75	2.20	2.20
	a	… imperforate		1.75		2.20
98	65f	1847 Mauritius – 1d & 2d "POST OFFICE" souvenir sheet (imperforate)[8]				
				2.25		2.80

92　　　　　　　　　　　　　　93

91　　　　　　94　　　　　　95　　　　　　96　　　　　　97

8　The 65f souvenir sheet (98) is often referred to as a miniature sheet. However, as the design cannot be reduced by perforation to display a smaller stamp, it must be regarded as a souvenir sheet with postal validity.

				£ MNH	£ FU/CTO	$US MNH	$US FU/CTO

1967   AMPHILEX – Philatelic Exhibition, Amsterdam

May 1967

99	75f	Tulips, windmills and USA "inverted Jenny".		.50	.50	.65	.65
a		... imperforate		2.75		3.50	
100	75f	miniature sheet		2.00		2.50	
a		... imperforate		12.50		15.50	

99

1967   Coronation of Sultan Ghalib bin Awadh al-Qu'aiti II

10 June 1967

101	25f	chocolate, silver & black	
102	100f	greenish black, gold & black	
103	250f	indigo, gold & black	
104	500f	maroon, gold & black	

101/104		set of 4		3.50		4.50
a		... imperforate		4.00		5.00

101   102   103   104

1967   Summer Olympics – Mexico City (2)

105	75f	deep lilac, yellow-olive & red		.85		1.05
a		... green, red-orange & violet (imperforate)		1.75		2.20
106	75f	miniature Sheet		2.25		2.80
a		... green, red-orange & violet (imperforate)		18.00		22.50

105   105a

			£ MNH	£ FU/CTO	$US MNH	$US FU/CTO

1967   Paintings

CTO stamps sighted dated 10 July 1967.

107	5f	*Master Hare*	Sir Joshua Reynolds
108	10f	*Self-portrait*	Albrecht Dürer
109	15f	*Anne of Cleves*	Hans Holbein the Younger
110	20f	*Francis I*	Jean Clouet
111	25f	*La Bohemienne*	Frans Hals
112	50f	*An Officer of the Imperial Horse Guard Charging*	Théodore Géricault
113	65f	*Prince Baltasar Carlos*	Diego Velázquez

			£ MNH	£ FU/CTO	$US MNH	$US FU/CTO
107/113		set of 7	2.50	2.50	3.10	3.10
a		... imperforate	3.00		3.75	
114	50f + 65f	miniature sheet	4.50		5.75	
a		... imperforate	20.00		25.00	

107   108   109   110   111   112   113

1967   12th World Scout Jamboree – Idaho, USA

August 1967

CTO stamps sighted dated 23 August 1967.

			£ MNH	£ FU/CTO	$US MNH	$US FU/CTO
115	35f	multicoloured	.60	.60	.75	.75
a		... imperforate	1.50		1.90	
116	35f	miniature sheet	2.00		2.50	
a		... imperforate	20.00		25.00	

115

1967   Winter Olympics – Grenoble, France

September 1967

CTO stamps sighted dated 28 September 1967

117	5f	Cross-country skiing
118	10f	Ice hockey
119	15f	Figure skating

120	20f	Downhill skiing				
121	25f	Speed skating				
122	35f	Two-man bob				
123	50f	Ski jump ramp				
124	65f	Ski jump				
117/124		set of 8	2.25	2.25	2.80	2.80
a		... imperforate	1.75		2.20	
125	50f + 65f	miniature sheet	7.00		8.75	
a		... imperforate	20.00		25.00	

 117
 119
 118
 120
 121

 122
 123
 124

1967 Space Exploration

October 1967
CTO stamps sighted dated 16 October 1967 (format 16.10.67 on two lines.)

126	10f	Saturn V launch				
127	25f	Space station project				
128	35f	Atlas Centaur rocket				
129	50f	Astronaut on surface of moon				
130	75f	Astronaut and Lunar Excursion Module (LEM)				
131	100f	Astronauts and lunar rover				
132	250f	Apollo capsule re-entering Earth's atmosphere				
126/132		set of 7	1.75	1.75	2.20	2.20
a		... imperforate	3.50		4.50	
133	100f + 250f	miniature sheet	6.00		7.50	
a		... imperforate	12.50		15.50	

 127
 129
 130

126 128 131 132

1967   Paintings – Edouard Manet

December 1967

CTO stamps sighted dated 23 December 1967.

134	10f	Woman with Parrot
135	35f	Boy with Cherries
136	50f	The Sultana
137	65f	Lola of Valence
138	75f	In the Greenhouse
139	200f	Nana
140	250f	A Bar at the Folies Bergere

134/140		set of 7	1.75	1.75	2.20	2.20
a		... imperforate	1.75		2.20	
141	250f	miniature sheet	1.75		2.20	
a		... imperforate	13.50		17.00	

134   135   136

137   138   139   140

Note: Images of miniature sheets are presented, at approximately half actual size, after the listings.

> **30 November 1967**
>
> Qu'aiti State became part of the People's Republic of Southern Yemen on 30 November 1967. The postal validity of all 1968 stamps is therefore in question. Given the lack of known 'issue' dates, some of the later 1967 stamps are also in doubt.

1967 — EXPO 67 – World's Fair, Montreal

December 1967

142	150f	Great Britain pavilion	1.25	1.25	1.60	1.60
a		... imperforate	1.75		2.20	
143	150f	miniature sheet	1.75	1.75	2.20	2.20
a		... imperforate	25.00		31.00	

142

1967 — 36th Monte Carlo Rally

December 1967

144	75f	multicoloured	.85	.85	1.05	1.05
a		... imperforate	1.25		1.60	
145	75f	miniature sheet	3.50		4.50	
a		... imperforate	15.00		19.00	

144

1967 — Painting – *Wolf Hunt*, Peter Paul Rubens

December 1967

146	75f	multicoloured	.85	.85	1.05	1.05
a		... imperforate	1.25		1.60	
147	75f	miniature sheet	3.50		4.50	
a		... imperforate	15.00		19.00	

146

				£ MNH	£ FU/CTO	$US MNH	$US FU/CTO

1967   Apollo 1 Astronauts Memorial

December 1967

				£ MNH	£ FU/CTO	$US MNH	$US FU/CTO
148	500f	Grissom, White and Chaffee		1.25	1.25	1.60	1.60
a		... imperforate		2.50		3.10	
149	500f	miniature sheet		2.50		3.10	
a		... imperforate		15.00		19.00	

148

1967   Paintings – Pierre-Auguste Renoir

CTO stamps sighted dated 6 January 1968.

150	25f	*The Clown*
151	100f	*Dance at Bougival*
152	150f	*The End of Breakfast*
153	500f	*Umbrellas*
154	500f	*Umbrellas* (larger detail of painting)

				£ MNH	£ FU/CTO	$US MNH	$US FU/CTO
150/153		set of 4		1.75	1.75	2.20	2.20
a		... imperforate		2.50		3.10	
155	500f	miniature sheet (no. 154)		1.75		2.20	
a		... imperforate		15.00		19.00	

150   151   152   153

1967   Paintings – Lucas Cranach the Elder

CTO stamps sighted dated 15 January 1968.

156	25f	*Henry the Pious, Duke of Saxony*
157	25f	*Wife of Duke Henry*
158	30f	*Dr Johannes Cuspinian*
159	30f	*Anna Cuspinian*
160	100f	*A Prince of Saxony*
161	100f	*A Princess of Saxony*
162	150f	*Emperor Maximilian*
163	150f	*Sixtus Oelhafen*

			£ MNH	£ FU/CTO	$US MNH	$US FU/CTO
164	500f	*Emperor Maximilian*				
165	500f	*Sixtus Oelhafen*				
156/163		set of 8 – gold frame	2.00	2.00	2.50	2.50
a		... silver frame	2.00		2.50	
aa		... ... imperforate	4.00		5.00	
166	500f + 500f	miniature sheet – gold frame	2.25		2.80	
a		... imperforate – silver frame	20.00		25.00	

156aa 157aa

158aa 159aa

160aa 161aa 162aa 163aa

1967   Paintings – Equestrian

167	10f	*Hunt of the Unicorn*	..unknown	
168	35f	*Francis I on Horseback*	..François Clouet	
169	50f	*Battle of San Romano*	..Paolo Uccello	
170	65f	*Riding in the Bois de Boulogne*	..Pierre-Auguste Renoir	
171	75f	*St Martin and the Beggar*	..El Greco	
172	200f	*Mounted Officer of the Imperial Guard* ...	..Théodore Géricault	
173	250f	*Allegory of April*	..Francesco del Cossa	

			£ MNH	£ FU/CTO	$US MNH	$US FU/CTO
167/173		set of 7 – gold frame	2.75	2.75	3.50	3.50
a		... silver frame	2.75		3.50	
b		... imperforate – silver frame	4.00		5.00	
174	250f	miniature sheet – gold frame	4.50		5.75	
a		... imperforate – silver frame	22.50		28.00	

167　　168　　169

170　　171　　172　　173

1967　　Paintings – Rembrandt van Rijn

175	25f	*The Night Watch I*				
176	250f	*The Night Watch II*				
177	500f	*The Night Watch III*				
175/177		set of 3 (se-tenant)	1.75	1.75	2.20	2.20
a		… imperforate	3.50		4.50	
178	500f	miniature sheet	2.25	2.25	2.80	2.80
a		… imperforate	10.00		12.50	

175　　176　　177

1967　　International Tourist Year – Paintings

179	10f	*The Morning Walk*	Thomas Gainsborough
180	35f	*Portrait of a Member of the Wedigh Family*	Hans Holbein
181	50f	*Infanta Margarita*	Diego Velázquez
182	65f	*Simonetta Vespucci*	Sandro Botticelli
183	75f	*The Syndics of the Clothmakers' Guild*	Rembrandt van Rijn

			£ MNH	£ FU/CTO	$US MNH	$US FU/CTO
184	100f	*The Clothed Maja* .... Francisco Goya				
185	150f	*Federico da Montefeltro* .... Piero della Francesca				
186	200f	*Ginevra de' Benci* .... Leonardo da Vinci				
179/186		set of 8	2.00	2.00	2.50	2.50
a		... 4 sheetlets (2 x 4 stamps each)	10.00		12.50	
b		... imperforate	5.00		6.25	
ba		... ... 4 sheetlets (2 x 4 stamps each)				
187	200f	miniature sheet	1.50		1.90	
a		... imperforate	22.00		27.50	

1968   Prehistoric and Modern Animals

188	5f	Sabre-tooth tiger				
189	5f	Leopards				
190	10f	Dinosaurs				
191	10f	Tylosaurus				
192	35f	Brontosaurus				
193	35f	Sharks				
194	50f	Mastodon				
195	50f	Rhinoceros				
196	65f	Kangaroos				
197	65f	Zebras				
198	75f	Ramphorhynchus				
199	75f	Condor				
200	200f	Chimpanzees				
201	200f	Early man				
202	250f	*Paradise* (Roelandt Savery)				
188/201		set of 14	4.25	4.25	5.25	5.25
a		... imperforate	6.00		7.50	
203	250f	miniature sheet	6.00		7.50	
a		... imperforate	20.00		25.00	

188/189 190/191 192/193

194/195 196/197 198/199 200/201

1968   Seven Wonders of the World, Ancient and Modern

204	10f	Statue of Zeus, Olympia				
205	10f	Giant Buddha, Kamakura				
206	35f	Hanging Gardens of Babylon				
207	35f	Spaceship on the Moon				
208	50f	Lighthouse at Alexandria				
209	50f	Eiffel Tower, Paris				
210	65f	Pyramids of Giza, Egypt				
211	65f	Mount Rushmore, USA				
212	75f	Tomb of Mausolus, Turkey				
213	75f	Leaning Tower of Pisa				
214	100f	Temple of Artemis, Ephesus				
215	100f	Taj Mahal, India				
216	200f	Colossus of Rhodes				
217	200f	Statue of Liberty, USA				
204/217		set of 14	5.00	5.00	6.25	6.25
a		... imperforate	5.00		6.25	
216/217 aa	2 x 200f	... ... inscriptions transposed				
216/217 b	2 x 200f	... inscriptions transposed				

204/205 206/207 208/209

210/211		212/213		214/215		216/217

218	2 x 200f	miniature sheet		6.00		7.50
a		… imperforate		15.00		19.00
aa		… … inscriptions transposed				
b		… inscriptions transposed				

1968 Ancient and Modern Olympic Games

219	5f	Wrestling
220	5f	Gymnastics (rings)
221	15f	Resting athlete
222	15f	Soccer
223	25f	Horseman
224	25f	Cyclist
225	500f	Discus
226	500f	Hurdler

219/226		set of 8	4.25	4.25		5.25	5.25
a		… imperforate	6.00			7.50	
227	500f + 500f	miniature sheet	6.00			7.50	
a		… imperforate	17.50			22.00	

219/220		221/222		223/224		225/226

1968 Aeroplanes and Spacecraft

Despite this series being regarded as a 1968 issue, CTO miniature sheets have been sighted dated 27 September 1967.

228	15f	1909 Louis Bleriot
229	15f	Veronique, French rocket
230	25f	1906 Santos Dumont, Brazil
231	25f	Vostok, last phase, USSR
232	100f	1896 Otto Lilienthal, Germany

			£ MNH	£ FU/CTO	$US MNH	$US FU/CTO
233	100f	Von Braun's rocket				
234	500f	1903 Wright Brothers, USA				
235	500f	Apollo rocket, last phases				
228/235		set of 8	4.50	4.50	5.75	5.75
a		... imperforate	6.00		7.50	
234 b	500f	... inscribed 1909 ENGLAND in error	40.00		50.00	
236	500f + 500f	miniature sheet	4.50	4.50	5.75	5.75
a		... imperforate	15.00		19.00	

  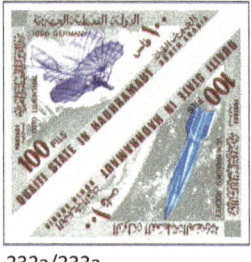 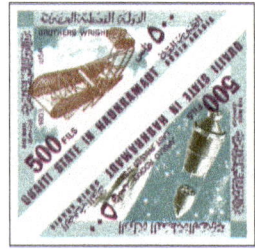

228a/229a   230a/231a   232a/233a   234a/235a

1968   EFIMEX – Philatelic Exhibition, Mexico City

Despite this stamp being regarded as a 1968 issue, CTO examples have been sighted dated 17 May 1967.

237	35f	Buildings and USA 1869 Columbus stamp	1.00	1.00	1.25	1.25
a		... imperforate	1.00		1.25	
238	35f	miniature sheet	3.50		4.50	
a		... imperforate	12.50		15.50	

237

◆

Qu'aiti State

Miniature Sheets

79 – World Cup Football Championship

81 – Summer Olympics – Mexico City (1)

90 – International Co-operation Year

98 (40% actual size) – STAMPEX

100a – AMPHILEX

106 – Summer Olympics – Mexico City (2)

114 – Paintings

116 – 12th World Scout Jamboree

125a – Winter Olympics – Grenoble, France

133 – Space Exploration

141 – Paintings – Edouard Manet

143 – EXPO 67

145 – 36th Monte Carlo Rally

147 – Painting – *Wolf Hunt*, Peter Paul Rubens

149a – Apollo 1 Astronauts Memorial

155 – Paintings – Auguste Renoir

166 – Paintings – Lucas Cranach

174a – Paintings – Equestrian

178a – Rembrandt van Rijn

187a – International Tourist Year, Paintings

203a – Prehistoric and Modern Animals

218a – Seven Wonders of the World

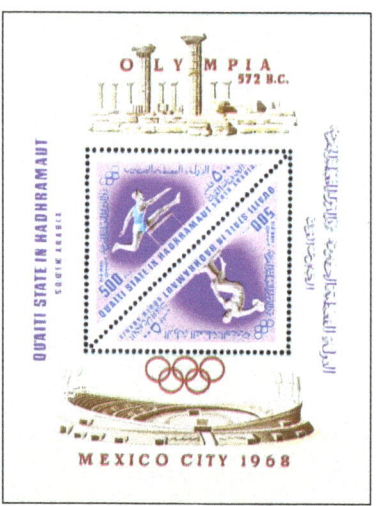
227 – Ancient and Modern Olympic Games

236 – Aeroplanes and Spacecraft

238 – EFIMEX

State of Upper Yafa

1967

1 – 10	Sep 1967	Definitives
11 – 17	Oct 1967	Summer Olympics – Mexico City
18 – 24	Oct 1967	Sculptures
25 – 32	Oct 1967	Paintings from the Louvre – Leonardo da Vinci
33 – 38	Oct 1967	World Cup Football Championship
39 – 50	Oct 1967	Paintings – Masters (1)
51 – 57	Oct 1967	Year of Human Rights / Kennedy Commemoration
58 – 64	Nov 1967	Paintings – Persian Miniatures
65 – 71	Nov 1967	Paintings – Edgar Degas
72 – 85	Nov 1967	Paintings – Masters (2)
86 – 95	Nov 1967	Winter Olympics – Grenoble
96 – 102	Nov 1967	20th Anniversary of UNICEF
103 – 109	Nov 1967	Paintings – Flowers

1967   **Definitives**

30 September 1967
First day covers have been sighted postmarked 1 October 1967.

1	5f	Flag of Upper Yafa and map
2	10f	Flag of Upper Yafa and map
3	20f	Flag of Upper Yafa and map
4	25f	Flag of Upper Yafa and map
5	40f	Flag of Upper Yafa and map
6	50f	Flag of Upper Yafa and map
7	75f	Emblem of Upper Yafa
8	100f	Emblem of Upper Yafa
9	250f	Emblem of Upper Yafa
10	500f	Emblem of Upper Yafa

1/10		set of 10	2.50	3.00

6

10

			£ MNH	£ FU/CTO	$US MNH	$US FU/CTO

1967   Summer Olympics – Mexico City

5 October 1967

11	15f	Olympic torch and sculpture of Coatlicue				
12	25f	Olympic torch and vase in the form of a man				
13	50f	Olympic torch and head				
14	75f	Olympic torch and figure of a man				
15	150f	Olympic torch and figure of coyote				
16	360f	Olympic torch and head				
11/15		set of 5	.85	.85	1.05	1.05
a		... imperforate	1.00	1.00	1.25	1.25
b		... sheetlet of 10	1.15	1.15	1.45	1.45
ba		... ... imperforate	1.15	1.15	1.45	1.45
17	360f	miniature sheet (imperforate)	1.15	1.15	1.45	1.45

11

12

13

14

15

1967   Sculptures

9 October 1967

18	10f	*David* .... Michelangelo				
19	30f	*Augustus Caesar*				
20	60f	*Moses* .... Michelangelo				
21	75f	*Discus thrower* .... Myron				
22	150f	*Pietà* .... Michelangelo				
23	360f	*Pietà* .... Michelangelo				
18/22		set of 5	1.15	1.15	1.45	1.45
a		... imperforate	1.15	1.15	1.45	1.45
b		... sheetlet of 10	1.75	1.75	2.20	2.20
ba		... ... imperforate	1.75	1.75	2.20	2.20
24	360f	miniature sheet (imperforate)	.85	.85	1.05	1.05

Note: Images of miniature sheets are presented, at approximately half actual size, after the listings.

		18	19	20	21	22

1967   Paintings from the Louvre – Leonardo da Vinci

9 October 1967

25	50f	Mona Lisa				
26	100f	Self portrait				
27	150f	Louvre Museum, Paris				
28	200f	Self portrait				
29	250f	Mona Lisa				
25/29		set of 5	.85	.85	1.05	1.05
a		... imperforate	.85	.85	1.05	1.05
b		... sheetlet of 10	1.25	1.25	1.60	1.60
ba		... ... imperforate	1.25	1.25	1.60	1.60
30	150f	miniature sheet	.85	.85	1.05	1.05
31	200f	miniature sheet	.85	.85	1.05	1.05
32	250f	miniature sheet	.85	.85	1.05	1.05

25	26	27	28	29

1967   World Cup Football Championship

15 October 1967

33	5f	Goalkeeper making save				
34	10f	Jules Rimet Cup and Wembley Stadium				
35	50f	Goalkeeper making save				
36	100f	Jules Rimet Cup and Wembley Stadium				
37	200f	Jules Rimet Cup and Wembley stadium				
33/36		set of 4	.90	.90	1.10	1.10
a		... imperforate	2.75		3.50	
38	200f	miniature sheet (imperforate)	1.50	1.50	1.90	1.90

| | | 33 | | | 34 | | | 35 | | | 36 | |

1967   Paintings – Masters (1)

15 October 1967

39	10f	*Singing Boy with a Flute*	Frans Hals
40	15f	*Old Woman Praying*	Nicolaes Maes
41	20f	*The Goldfinch*	Carel Fabritius
42	25f	*The Sentry*	Carel Fabritius
43	30f	*Young Woman Doing Needlework*	Nicolaes Maes
44	40f	*A Dutch Courtyard*	Pieter de Hooch
45	50f	*Self-portrait as a Young Man*	Rembrandt van Rijn
46	60f	*Windmill Near Wijk*	Jacob van Ruisdael
47	75f	*Self-portrait*	Rembrandt van Rijn
48	150f	*Banquet of Officers of the Civic Guard of St. George*	Frans Hals

39/48		set of 10		.90	.90	1.10	1.10
a		... imperforate		.90	.90	1.10	1.10
39/43 b	10f - 30f	... sheetlet of 10		1.15	1.15	1.45	1.45
ba		... ... imperforate		1.15	1.15	1.45	1.45
44/48 b	40f - 150f	... sheetlet of 10		1.15	1.15	1.45	1.45
ba		... ... imperforate		1.15	1.15	1.45	1.45
49	50f	miniature sheet (imperforate)		.85	.85	1.05	1.05
50	150f	miniature sheet (imperforate)		.85	.85	1.05	1.05

| 39a | 40a | 41a | 42a | 43a |
| 44a | 45a | 46a | 47a | 48a |

				£ MNH	£ FU/CTO	$US MNH	$US FU/CTO

1967 — Year of Human Rights / Kennedy Commemoration

30 October 1967

No.	Value	Description		£ MNH	£ FU/CTO	$US MNH	$US FU/CTO
51	5f	Kennedy and Flame of Liberty					
52	10f	Kennedy in rocking chair					
53	50f	Kennedy's grave, Arlington Cemetery					
54	75f	Kennedy in rocking chair					
55	125f	Kennedy and Flame of Liberty					
56	180f	Kennedy and Flame of Liberty					
51/55		set of 5		.50	.50	.65	.65
a		... imperforate		.50	.50	.65	.65
b		... sheetlet of 10		.85	.85	1.05	1.05
ba		... ... imperforate		.85	.85	1.05	1.05
57	180f	miniature sheet (imperforate)		1.15	1.15	1.45	1.45

51a 52a 53a 54a 55a

1967 — Paintings – Persian Miniatures

3 November 1967

No.	Value	Description		£ MNH	£ FU/CTO	$US MNH	$US FU/CTO
58	10f	*Hunting Scene*					
59	20f	*Landscape with Crow, Turtle and Antelope*					
60	30f	*Landscape with Rider and Parrot*					
61	40f	*Lion Killing an Ass*					
62	50f	*War Scene*					
63	180f	*Hunting Scene*					
58/62		set of 5		.60	.60	.75	.75
a		... imperforate		.60	.60	.75	.75
b		... sheetlet of 10		1.10	1.10	1.40	1.40
ba		... ... imperforate		1.10	1.10	1.40	1.40
64	180f	miniature sheet (imperforate)		.85	.85	1.05	1.05

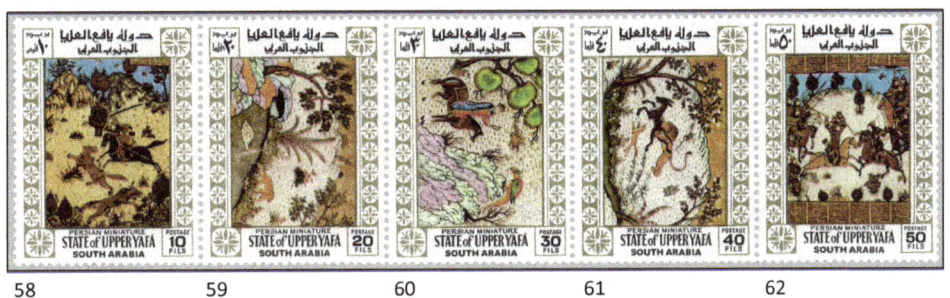

58 59 60 61 62

			£ MNH	£ FU/CTO	$US MNH	$US FU/CTO

1967   Paintings – Edgar Degas

3 November 1967

65	20f	*Ballet Dancers* I				
66	30f	*Ballet Dancers* II				
67	40f	*Ballet Dancers* III				
68	50f	*Ballet Dancers* IV				
69	60f	*Ballet Dancers* V				
70	180f	*Ballet Dancers* I				
65/69		set of 5	.70	.70	.90	.90
a		… imperforate	.70	.70	.90	.90
b		… sheetlet of 10	.85	.85	1.05	1.05
ba		… … imperforate	1.10	1.10	1.40	1.40
71	180f	miniature sheet (imperforate)	.85	.85	1.05	1.05

65a   66a   67a   68a   69a

1967   Paintings – Masters (2)

15 November 1967

72	25f	*Portrait of Maddalena Strozzi* … … … … … Raphael				
73	50f	*Joanna of Aragon* … … … … … … … … … Raphael				
74	75f	*Don Manuel Osorio de Zúñiga* … … … … Francisco Goya				
75	100f	*The Cumaean Sibyl* … … … … … … … Domenichino				
76	125f	*Pope Innocent X* … … … … … … … … Diego Velázquez				
77	150f	*Boy with a Basket of Fruit* … … … … … Michelangelo Merisi da Caravaggio				
78	175f	*The Blue Boy* … … … … … … … … … Thomas Gainsborough				
79	200f	*Doña Isabel Cobos de Porcel* … … … … Francisco Goya				
80	225f	*The Fifer* … … … … … … … … … … … Édouard Manet				
81	250f	*Sick Bacchus* … … … … … … … … … Michelangelo Merisi da Caravaggio				
82	500f	*Don Manuel Osorio de Zúñiga* … … … … Francisco Goya				
83	500f	*Sick Bacchus* … … … … … … … … … Michelangelo Merisi da Caravaggio				
72/81		set of 10	.90	.90	1.10	1.10
a		… imperforate	.90	.90	1.10	1.10
72/76 b		… sheetlet of 10	1.15	1.15	1.45	1.45
77/81 b		… sheetlet of 10	1.15	1.15	1.45	1.45
84	500f	miniature sheet (*Don Manuel*) imperforate	.85	.85	1.05	1.05
85	500f	miniature sheet (*Sick Bacchus*) imperforate	.85	.85	1.05	1.05

72a 73a 74a 75a 76a

77a 78a 79a 80a 81a

1967   Winter Olympics – Grenoble, France

25 November 1967

The World Cup Football Championship set (33 – 36) overprinted with the following logo in the colours indicated.

86	5f	silver & green
87	5f	gold & blue
88	10f	silver & green
89	10f	gold & blue
90	50f	silver & green
91	50f	gold & blue
92	100f	silver & green
93	100f	gold & blue
94	200f	violet & green

86/93		set of 8	3.00	3.75
a		… imperforate	3.00	3.75
b		… overprint inverted	25.00	30.00
aa		… … imperforate / overprint inverted	25.00	30.00
95	200f	miniature sheet (imperforate)	2.50	3.10

1967   20th Anniversary of the UNICEF

25 November 1967

96	50f	*Infanta Margarita Teresa*	Diego Velázquez
97	75f	*Young Peasant Boy*	Bartolomé Murillo
98	100f	*Portrait of Mademoiselle Legrand*	Pierre-Auguste Renoir
99	125f	*Portrait of a Young Girl*	Pierre-Auguste Renoir
100	250f	*Portrait of Yvonne Grimpel*	Pierre-Auguste Renoir
101	360f	*Young Peasant Boy*	Bartolomé Murillo

			£ MNH	£ FU/CTO	$US MNH	$US FU/CTO
96/100		set of 5	.70	.70	.90	.90
	a	... imperforate	.70	.70	.90	.90
	b	... sheetlet of 10	1.10	1.10	1.40	1.40
	ba	... ... imperforate	1.10	1.10	1.40	1.40
102	360f	miniature sheet (imperforate)	1.15	1.15	1.45	1.45

96a 97a 98a 99a 100a

1967 Paintings – Flowers

25 November 1967

103	5f	*Flowers in a Glass Vase*	Jacob van Walscapelle
104	10f	*Chrysanthemums in a Vase*	Pierre-Auguste Renoir
105	50f	*Vase with Fourteen Sunflowers*	Vincent Van Gogh
106	100f	*Flowers in a Vase*	Paulus van Brussel
107	150f	*Flowers in a Vase*	Paulus van Brussel
108	180f	*Chrysanthemums in a Vase*	Pierre-Auguste Renoir

			£ MNH	£ FU/CTO	$US MNH	$US FU/CTO
103/107		set of 5	.90	.90	1.10	1.10
	a	... imperforate	.90	.90	1.10	1.10
	b	... sheetlet of 10	1.25	1.25	1.60	1.60
	ba	... ... imperforate	1.25	1.25	1.60	1.60
109	180f	miniature sheet (imperforate)	1.00	1.00	1.25	1.25

103 104 105 106 107

◆

State of Upper Yafa

Miniature Sheets

17 – Summer Olympics, Mexico City

24 – Sculptures

30 – Louvre, Paris

31 – da Vinci self-portrait

32 – da Vinci, Mona Lisa

38 – World Cup Football Championship

49 – Paintings, Masters (1), Rembrandt

50 – Paintings, Masters (1), Hals

57 – Year of Human Rights / John Kennedy

64 – Paintings, Persian Miniatures

71 – Paintings, Degas

84 – Paintings, Masters (2), Goya

85 – Paintings, Masters (2), Michelangelo

102 – UNICEF

109 – Paintings, Flowers, Renoir

◆

BIBLIOGRAPHY

The editor gratefully acknowledges the following resources:

Aden Specialized Catalog
  Philatelics Unlimited (1987)

Catalogue of Queen Elizabeth II Postage Stamps
  John Lister Limited (1971)

Commonwealth & British Empire Stamps 1840-1970
  Stanley Gibbons (2018)

Commonwealth Five Reigns
  Bridger & Kay Ltd (1980)

Commemorative Stamps of the British Commonwealth
  H.D.S. Haverbeck
  Faber and Faber (1955)

Dhow, The
  Aden & Somaliland Study Group (various editions, 2000 to 2022)

Elizabethan Specialised Catalogue of Modern British Commonwealth Stamps
  Stanley Gibbons (various editions)

Gulf States Catalogue 2013 – 2nd edition
  Michel (2013)

Philatelic Magazine, The – Vol. 57, No. 15
  Harris Publications Ltd. (22 July 1949)

Potter-Shelton Tables of K.G. VI Printings
  Stamp Collecting Ltd (1997)

Two Reigns Postage Stamp Catalogue
  Stanley Gibbons (1964)

www.ingramcontent.com/pod-product-compliance
Lightning Source LLC
Chambersburg PA
CBHW061134010526
44107CB00068B/2931